The Uncommon Leader:

10 Laws of Leadership

Praise for *The Uncommon Leader*

David Baxter's impact extends far beyond auditoriums and conference rooms. He's a catalyst for change, sparking revolutions and mindset in action.

—Chicago Weekly

Most leadership books lean on theory, but David Baxter's wisdom is forged in the fires of real adversity. Having risen from challenges that would break most, he's turned his hard-won lessons into leadership tools that resonate in any industry. This book doesn't just offer advice; it serves the full meal, and it's a game-changer for anyone ready to elevate their leadership to the next level.

—Jeremy Anderson, CEO of The Jeremy Anderson Group, CEO/Founder of the Next Level Speakers Academy, Founder of Next Level Living Inc.

One of the most essential leadership books of the decade, The Uncommon Leader rips away corporate clichés and reveals the truth: real leadership can be forged from the most unexpected places.

—Julie Bishop, international bestselling author of *Thrive Away*

A masterclass in resiliency and true leadership, The Uncommon Leader gives the resources you need to thrive in any environment.

—Andrew Litchfield, CEO of Penny Investments

In a time when we need more leaders of action, not words, Baxter's book is a great resource.

—Josh Kraft, President of the New England Patriots Foundation

David Baxter's vision, perseverance, and leadership are an inspiration. His work is helping make our prisons, communities, and streets safer for everyone. The Uncommon Leader is not just a guide for returning citizens, but for anyone seeking to give back and help build a more peaceful society.

—Jamie Eldridge, Massachusetts State Senator, Chair, Joint Committee on Revenue, Vice Chair, Joint Committee on the Judiciary, and Joint Committee on State Administration and Regulatory Oversight

The Uncommon Leader *presents a definitive examination of leadership grounded in responsibility, character, and purpose. David Baxter articulates principles that reflect the enduring demands of leadership.*

—Lee Pelton, CEO of The Boston Foundation

Most leadership books talk about adversity. David Baxter comes from it. He studied it. Then he engineered it into a practical blueprint for influence, resilience, and purpose. The Uncommon Leader does not offer theory; it offers tools. As someone raised in Brooklyn's Bedford-Stuyvesant who later led a district to a 100% graduation rate, I recognize leadership that actually works in real-world conditions. This book delivers.

—Anael "Dr. A" Alston, Former Superintendent, New York State Principal of the Year

David Baxter doesn't write about adversity from a distance; he writes from experience. The Uncommon Leader is built on earned credibility, where the journey from streets to suites is not a slogan, but a lived reality. That authenticity gives this book a moral authority few leadership books can claim.

—Wilene Dunn, CEO of WCD Enterprises

The Uncommon Leader:

10 Laws of Leadership

Essential Skills from the Streets to the Suites: Proven Strategies to Inspire, Motivate, and Build Exceptionally Successful Teams in Any Environment

DAVID BAXTER

DREAMERS
PUBLISHING

Published in the United States by Dreamers Publishing, an imprint of Dreamers Media LLC, Boston

ISBN: 979-8-9957703-0-5 (paperback)

ISBN: 979-8-9957703-1-2 (hardcover)

ISBN: 979-8-9957703-2-9 (ebook)

First Edition, THE UNCOMMON LEADER, 10 LAWS OF LEADERSHIP

Cover design by Julie Bishop & Greferente

Cover production by Damonza

Font: Minion Pro

CONTENTS

To my loving mother, thank you for the values you instilled in me and for showing me what unconditional love truly looks and feels like.

And

To my one and only daughter Tyonna, I love you more than the air that keeps me breathing. Thanks for being my "why" that carried me through my darkest hours.

ACKNOWLEDGMENTS

This book wouldn't exist without the lessons, love, and light I received along the way. Some of you helped me bring these pages to life. Others helped bring me back to life. I want to honor both.

First and foremost, I want to acknowledge my higher power, God, because through You, all things are possible. I am living proof of that.

To the mother of my only child, Teisha. Thank you for blessing me with the greatest gift God can bestow: fatherhood. And thank you for holding everything together while I was away, figuring out this thing called life.

Next, I want to thank international bestselling author Julie Bishop for being a guiding light throughout this process. You were a steady beacon throughout this process, helping me navigate the paralysis of writer's block, stay on course, and ultimately cross the finish line. Without you, this book would not exist. I am eternally and humbly grateful for your guidance, mentorship, and for the immeasurable honor of calling you my friend.

To Kerryn Fernandes, there are no words that can truly capture the love I have for you. You were my brightest light during the darkest season of my life. That is something I will never forget and carry in my heart forever. I will always be grateful.

I would like to thank my beta readers: Francine Johnson, Ruth Zachary, Natalie Sciallo, Lynn French, and Gail McDonald. Thank you for your time, your willingness, and your patience in reading my book. Your candid feedback and thoughtful insight made this the strongest version it could be. Your contributions have been invaluable.

To my editors, Johanna P. Leigh, Alexa Nazario, Ayessha Paarkar, and Rachel Ross, I thank you for your extraordinary patience, your consummate wisdom, and for generously sharing your years of expertise with me in a field entirely new to me. Your dedication and insight have shaped this book in ways I could not have achieved on my own. I am profoundly grateful for your guidance and for helping me bring this vision to life.

To all the remarkable mentors and coaches who have shaped my journey: Rakim McGirt, Mac Hudson, Minister Randy Muhammad, Tony Robbins, Ed Bastian, Jeremy Anderson, Andrew Litchfield, Dr. Eric E.T. Thomas, and others. Each of you has poured into me at pivotal moments and in profoundly different and meaningful ways. You have shaped my business philosophy, my personal life philosophy, and helped me become not only the leader, but the man I am today. I humbly thank you for your guidance, your wisdom, and for believing in my potential long before I fully believed in it myself.

To Betsy Chace, thank you for being the best friend and confidant one could ever ask for. Thank you for setting me straight without hesitation, never holding back punches when you disagreed with me, and for always believing in me. Your honesty, love, and steadfast support have been unwavering, and I am deeply grateful to have you in my life.

To Megan Boyer, a.k.a. Dimples, thank you for your love and support throughout this process. Thank you for providing both the emotional and physical space I needed to work through this book, and for doing your best to understand my journey. I am thankful for your presence in my life and for your support every step of the way.

To my dear friend and partner in vision, Rachel Balian. Thank you for the behind-the-scenes work you do, the kind that often goes unnoticed yet makes so many aspects of Motivational Dreamers appear effortless. Without you, much of what we've built would not have been possible.

To every Fortune 500 company, nonprofit, university, K-12 school, and conference that trusted my vision and expertise with your staff or audience, I humbly thank you. This trust is never taken lightly, and I hope you've gained just as much insight and wisdom from me as I've gained from you. I cherish our partnerships and steward them with the utmost care and love.

To my Roca, Inc family, thank you for allowing me to call Roca home throughout this journey. Thank you for embracing me wholeheartedly, for trusting me, and for welcoming me into the fabric of what Roca truly stands for: changing the lives of countless young men and women through unwavering commitment, belief, and unconditional love.

To my Roca Boston youth, Tre. Thank you for holding me accountable for writing this book. Every time you saw me, you embodied relentlessness, holding me to deadlines, and I appreciate it more than words will ever adequately convey.

To my entire team at Motivational Dreamers and every other initiative I have brought to life, I thank you with every fiber of my being. While I may be on the stages and in the rooms, it is you who do the heavy lifting to make my dreams a reality. I will forever be indebted and grateful for your tireless dedication, love, and belief in this vision.

And last, but certainly not least, to all the Uncommon Leaders out there. From top executives shaping companies to young men and women just starting out, figuring out their purpose, finding their way in classrooms, neighborhoods, or the quiet of their own homes—this book is for you. May it serve as your guide, your compass, and your encouragement to step boldly into the leader you are meant to be.

FOREWORD

What constitutes real leadership? This may be the most important question of our time. Trust in leaders is at an all-time low. We witness daily the misuse of power and authority, along with constant attempts to redefine leadership to fit personal agendas. In an era marked by devastating wars, widespread corruption, rising homelessness and hunger, and shifting global alliances, the need for positive, compassionate, and values-driven leadership has never been greater.

True leadership can arise from both formal authority and personal character. It is the conscious decision to use one's platform and influence to help others, to do what is right even when it is difficult, and to build stronger companies, healthier communities, and a more prosperous world. This is why The Uncommon Leader is not just relevant—it is essential for anyone in a position of authority or anyone seeking to positively influence others.

David Baxter developed his approach to leadership from hard-earned experience: lessons learned on the streets, during his time in prison, through mentors, extensive reading, and conversations with people from all walks of life—from at-risk youth to community leaders to corporate executives. Using these experiences, he distilled Ten Laws of Leadership—a practical framework for becoming an exceptional leader.

But this book is far more than one man's story. It demonstrates that leadership is not reserved for those with titles, pedigree, or formal power. It is forged through conscious choices, personal accountability, reflection, and the willingness to grow. Leadership emerges precisely in the moments when it would be easier to look away or make the expedient choice, yet one chooses to step forward in these difficult, uncertain, or uncomfortable circumstances.

In these pages, you will see leadership in its rawest form. You will learn that failure is not something to hide from, but a powerful teacher. You will discover how communication, trust, discipline, and purpose become practical tools that drive real results—whether on the streets, in prison, or in the corporate boardroom.

Being honest with ourselves is never easy, particularly when we have fallen short in the domain of values, the law, or organizational standards. David courageously pulls back the curtain on his own struggles with ego, morality, and the consequences of his actions on others. Through his Ten Laws of Leadership, he invites us to examine our own lives and make better choices.

The Uncommon Leader is David Baxter's timely gift to all of us. Navigating unprecedented challenges to our safety, health, and economic security—while harnessing the immense opportunities created by technological innovation—will demand uncommonly strong leaders at every level of government, business, and the nonprofit sector. I hope this book engages your mind and challenges you to rise to that standard as much as it did for me. Your friends, neighbors, co-workers, and fellow citizens are counting on you.

Molly Baldwin
Founder & CEO, Roca, Inc.

AUTHOR'S NOTE:

Some of the work, milestones, and stories referenced in this book took place under Motivational Dreamers, the original name of my company. Since completing this book, the company now operates as David Baxter & Associates. While the name has evolved, the mission and work remain the same.

*A leader is best when people
barely know he exists.
When his work is done,
his aim fulfilled, they will
say: we did it ourselves.*

—Lao Tzu

INTRODUCTION

From the Streets to the Suite

When you hear the word "leadership," you might picture executives in boardrooms, polished suits, armed with Ivy League degrees and impressive résumés. Yet what if I told you that some of the most profound lessons in leadership aren't only found in corporate offices or prestigious universities; they're also born in the harsh realities of the streets? My name is David Baxter, and my journey to leadership has been anything but conventional.

I grew up in the Bedford-Stuyvesant section of Brooklyn, during the height of the violent crack epidemic, with my mother and three siblings. The odds were stacked against me: fatherless home, poverty, violence, and the constant pull of the streets. The streets became my first classroom, teaching me hard but vital lessons about survival, adaptability, and the power of human connection. That resilience, forged in chaos, would later shape the way I lead.

From an early age, my mother instilled in me the profound value of education, not just through words but through her own relentless pursuit of knowledge. As a full-time mother of four, she balanced a career while advancing her education, earning multiple degrees. She was a living testament to perseverance and dedication.

I excelled in school, but at fourteen, I made a reckless choice. I became involved in a racially charged brawl at my high school, a decision that led to my expulsion. That turning point marked the moment when the streets, with all their dangers and influences, began to take hold of me.

Despite my love for education, being expelled sent me into a rebellious phase. My mother went to great lengths to enroll me in another school, but I refused, not out of disrespect or lack of love, but from fear of the unknown. I wasn't ready to leave the familiar comforts of my neighborhood and friends. So instead of school, my days were spent hanging out in the neighborhood, until the day arrived that would define the next chapter of my life: Rakim.

By the age of twenty, I was leading a million-dollar drug empire that spanned the East Coast: Massachusetts, Tennessee, Maryland, New York, Virginia, and Vermont. It was a life of private and first-class flights, fast cars, lavish homes, and endless parties with music celebrities. At the time, I thought I had mastered success.

But the streets have a way of reminding you that no empire built on sand can stand forever. It all came crashing down when I was arrested by local, state, and federal authorities in 2003 and convicted in 2004. The Massachusetts prison system became my new reality. From private jets to steel bars, the contrast was suffocating.

But what might surprise you is that my rise in the criminal world wasn't just luck or ruthlessness. It was grounded in universal principles of leadership. Whether you're leading a team in the streets or sitting at the head of a corporate boardroom, the same core principles apply: influence, strategy, discipline, and commitment. The very principles that once fueled my street empire now drive my work in legitimate business.

After my fall, I found myself behind bars, where I took on a new leadership role within gang culture, growing our numbers into the largest single gang in Massachusetts. But as my sentence progressed, something shifted. Through mentorship and self-education, I began to question not only my path but the very essence of leadership. Inside those walls, I wrestled with fear, regret, and hope, and deep reflection revealed the importance of self-knowledge, restorative justice, forgiveness, and the power of believing in people. I came to understand that while power and influence could get you far, true leadership demanded something more: purpose. It isn't about controlling others, but about empowering them to rise. That revelation reshaped me both mentally and spiritually.

Transforming my mindset and behavior wasn't easy. It was a relentless battle—both internal and external. I wish I could say the change was simple or happened overnight, but it required deep spiritual and personal growth. I had to be intentional about my environment, surrounding myself with people who challenged me to grow—both inside and outside prison. I learned to see moments of relapse not as failures but as lessons, refusing to let setbacks define me. Education—both self-education and formal learning—became my foundation, each shaping me in ways I never could have imagined. Every step was critical in rewiring my thinking and, ultimately, transforming my life.

When I eventually left prison, I didn't abandon the leadership principles that had once fueled my success in the underworld. Instead, I realized those same principles could be transformed to uplift, inspire, and build something positive and enduring. I embraced those lessons and began using them to lead with purpose in the business world.

Today, as the founder and CEO of Motivational Dreamers, the TEARS organization, and co-founder of the No Longer 3/5th Coalition, I've taken those same leadership principles and use them to help nonprofits, universities, small companies, and Fortune 500 giants unlock the power of leadership through real-world, practical experience, not just theoretical knowledge.

Through these experiences, I've seen firsthand that leadership isn't about titles or corner offices; it's about influence, integrity, and the courage to do what's right, even when it's hard. These are the principles I'll show you how to apply in this book.

The Ten Laws of Leadership

Through my journey, I've distilled ten critical laws of leadership that are essential for success, no matter what your background or industry. These ten laws: lead with purpose, embrace failure, master communication, celebrate success, honor commitments, moral courage, actively listen, develop others to lead, anchor in wisdom, and lead beyond yourself, form the foundation of this book.

While these concepts are familiar to many, few truly understand them, and even fewer know how to implement them successfully. They're the same principles that guided me from the streets to the suite, and they continue to shape my work today.

This book isn't about conventional leadership theory; it's about leadership forged in the fire of life's hardest experiences. I've seen these principles work in the most extreme environments imaginable, and I know they can work for you, too.

Whether you're an executive leading a corporate team or a university, an entrepreneur starting a business, or a community leader striving to make a difference, these ten laws of leadership will give you the tools to inspire, motivate, and lead others with integrity and purpose.

From Crime to Corporate: How I Lead Today

I am often asked how someone with my background can stand before CEOs, executives, and community leaders and talk about leadership. The answer is simple: I've lived it, in ways most leaders haven't. My knowledge doesn't come from books, theories, surveys, or secondhand stories. It comes from experience.

I've been homeless and had to survive and overcome that. I've built million-dollar empires from nothing—both in the streets and in the business world. I know what it means to lose everything and still have the resilience, heart, determination, and patience to rebuild from the ground up.

I've led teams of five and teams of one hundred. I've mentored formidable individuals in the streets and managers and executives from organizations of all sizes. I've worked with people from all walks of life, including leaders, entrepreneurs, and everyday individuals who strive for something greater.

Yes, I also have the degrees and credentials from top institutions, but the lessons I speak about, the kind that shape a different kind of leadership, can't be taught in a classroom. My credibility wasn't earned through theory or a piece of paper. It was forged in the fire of the greatest teacher of all: life.

Growing and leading a million-dollar empire in the streets, to leading at a military-style academy, to later leading a gang, and now being a leader in the business world has taught me that leadership is universal. Whether you're leading in the streets or in business, the same core principles apply.

But the turning point in my life came not from my rise in the criminal world but from my fall. It was in prison that I began to refine and redefine what leadership meant within a positive, productive context. Within those walls, I came to understand what it means to lead with purpose. I learned that while power and success can be achieved through sheer will, true leadership is about something deeper: lifting others, building trust, and creating an impact that lasts.

The strategies that once fueled my criminal empire are now helping legitimate organizations grow and thrive. I've seen firsthand how listening to your team, celebrating successes, honoring commitments, and communicating clearly can build a culture of loyalty and trust, whether you're leading a Fortune 500 company or a nonprofit.

Why I Wrote This Book

For years, I've been encouraged by people from all walks of life, including executives I've consulted, community leaders I've mentored, and even friends and family, to write a book sharing my unique insights on leadership. But it wasn't until I began working with more and more leaders that I realized the true need for this book

Despite their best intentions, many leaders struggled with blind spots that held back their potential: gaps in communication, failure to embrace mistakes, and lack of trust within teams. The more I witnessed this, the more I realized that my story and the leadership lessons I've learned could help others avoid those same pitfalls.

Working with organizations of all sizes, from grassroots nonprofits to Fortune 500 companies, has taught me one undeniable truth:

leadership isn't measured by the size of your title or the office you occupy, but by the tangible impact you create in the lives of others. That's what this book is about: turning experience into action.

From mentoring youth and students to consulting with CEOs, I've seen leaders rise and falter. The difference? Those who understand that leadership is about lifting others, not just driving numbers. In these pages, I'll share how to take the lessons I've learned and use them to create lasting change in any environment.

I wrote this book because, although I can't personally consult with every leader, I can share my experiences, insights, and solutions through these pages. My goal is to empower you to become a better, more impactful leader, whether you're just starting out or are already leading at a high level.

Throughout this book, you'll gain practical insights and strategies based on the ten key laws of leadership that have shaped my journey:

- Lead with Purpose
- Embrace Failure
- Master Communication
- Celebrate Success
- Moral Courage
- Honor Commitments
- Actively Listen
- Develop Others to Lead
- Anchor in Wisdom
- Lead Beyond Yourself

These are the laws of leadership that have taken me from the streets to the business world, and if you apply them, they can take you anywhere you want to go.

Leadership isn't about titles, degrees, or positions. It's about the positive change you create in the lives of others. My hope is that this book will not only inspire you but also equip you with the tools to become a more effective, thoughtful, and impactful leader.

So, let's embark on this journey together and uncover the uncommon leader within you.

The function of leadership is to produce more leaders, not more followers.

—Ralph Nader

CHAPTER 1

LEAD WITH PURPOSE — EMPOWER OTHERS TO RISE

Ignite the Spark of Empowerment

In every corner of life, from the tough streets of Bedford-Stuyvesant to the corridors of corporate America, true leadership isn't about wielding power; it's about lighting the way for others to rise. This chapter isn't a manual on command and control; it's a call to embrace leadership rooted in purpose, compassion, and the drive to empower others.

Here, you'll discover that the essence of leadership is found in everyday acts of lifting others, a lesson first taught by the unwavering love of a mother and later refined on the streets by mentors who led not through fear but through respect and empathy. Leadership is the journey of turning hardship into shared vision and setbacks into stepping stones toward collective progress.

As you step into these pages, prepare to challenge conventional notions of power. Embrace the idea that to lead with purpose is to serve selflessly, build bridges of trust, and cultivate a legacy where every voice is valued and every life uplifted. Welcome to a new paradigm of leadership, one that ignites empowerment in every heart it touches.

The foundation of true leadership is often seen as a title, a position, or a set of strategies for success. But I learned early that leadership is deeper: it's about influence, resilience, and an unwavering commitment to serving and elevating others.

My journey from the streets of Bedford-Stuyvesant to corporate America taught me that leadership isn't defined by the environment but by how you use your power to inspire and advance the position of others.

The Power of Purpose

In a world where survival often meant putting yourself first, I saw many rise by exploiting others. But I also saw a different kind of power rooted in respect, loyalty, and the genuine desire to uplift.

This kind of leadership didn't come from fear or intimidation; it came from love and a sense of purpose. John Hope Bryant refers to this as "Love Leadership." It's this purpose-driven leadership I want to share with you because it transforms not just organizations, but lives.

My mother, Janie, was the first leader I ever knew. A single mother raising four children in Brooklyn during the crack epidemic, she had every reason to focus on her own survival, but she chose to focus on us. She instilled in her kids the values of hard work, education, and family. Her leadership wasn't about demanding respect; it was about earning it through sacrifice, consistency, life lessons, and deep purpose.

One day, when I was about ten, my mother and my oldest brother, Andrew, had a disagreement. As the youngest, I naturally sided with her, thinking I was being loyal. Later that day, Andrew got tangled in a mess of bikes in my sister's room. Despite his calls for help, I ignored him, still "mad" on my mother's behalf. My mother noticed and quickly corrected me: "Boy, go help your brother."

When I returned, she said, "That is your brother. You and he are family. In life, you won't always get along, maybe even be mad at each other. None of that matters. Family sticks together in times of need. You're supposed to love him unconditionally, as I love you all unconditionally."

That day, my mother taught me a simple yet profound lesson: true leadership isn't about feelings, grudges, or proving a point; it's about taking responsibility for others. In that moment, she reframed what it meant to be part of something bigger than myself. It wasn't about winning an argument; it was about showing up, even when it was inconvenient or uncomfortable. That's the essence of leading with purpose.

As I grew older and stepped into leadership roles, I realized that the same principle applied far beyond our Brooklyn home. Leading with purpose means placing the mission, the people, and the greater good ahead of ego or fleeting emotions. It means lifting others, even those we might disagree with, because leadership is not about personal battles but about collective progress.

In organizations, communities, and life, there will always be conflict. There will be moments when pride tells us to turn away, to let someone struggle because we feel justified in our frustration. But a true leader, one who leads with purpose, understands that leadership is about service. Just as my mother showed me that love is not conditional, leadership, too, must not be driven by conditions. It must be anchored in a commitment to empowering others, even in moments of disagreement or difficulty.

Empowering Others Through Leadership

In the streets, leadership often gets a bad rap. It's seen as a way to gain power, respect, or wealth. There's some truth to that, just like on Wall Street. But the most respected leaders I knew, both in the streets and in corporate America, weren't the ones with the most money or the ones most feared. They were the ones who used their influence to better the lives of others.

Fear and respect are often mistaken for one another in leadership, both in the streets and in corporate America. On the surface, they look similar; both command obedience and establish authority. But they're fundamentally different in nature and impact on those being led.

Fear forces compliance; respect inspires commitment. Fear may get people to follow orders, but it does so by leveraging intimidation, control, and the threat of consequences. It creates a culture of silence, hesitation, and self-preservation, where people do only what is necessary to avoid punishment. Leadership through fear is transactional; it demands results but does not cultivate loyalty. The moment the source of fear is removed, so is the obedience.

Respect, on the other hand, is earned through integrity, consistency, and genuine care for those you lead. It fosters trust, inspires people to give their best, and builds a foundation where individuals feel valued, empowered, and driven by something greater than fear of consequence. Leadership rooted in respect doesn't just command; it uplifts. It creates an environment where people want to follow, not because they must, but because they believe in the leader and the vision they represent.

The greatest distinction is this: fear controls, but respect empowers. Fear weakens a team over time, while respect strengthens it. A leader who rules through fear may achieve short-term success, but a leader who leads with respect will build something that lasts.

Growing up, I only knew one style of leadership: fear. Intimidation, aggression, and the willingness to commit violence weren't just tools; they were the currency of respect. The biggest, boldest, most ruthless figures were admired and obeyed. And for young minds like mine, that became the blueprint. I believed that respect meant fear. That idea, unfortunately, shaped my view of manhood for years. Anything else was seen as weakness, and in the hood, weakness made you prey.

But I started noticing a pattern. The men who led through fear never lasted. No matter how powerful, their reign was always temporary. One by one, they fell, victims of the same violence they once used to control others. What struck me most wasn't just their deaths but the reaction to them. When these kings of the streets were taken out, the neighborhood didn't grieve. No real mourning, no deep sense of loss. Instead, there was relief—a weight lifted. That was my first glimpse into the reality that fear doesn't build legacies; it buries them.

It was in this realization that the first cracks formed in my understanding of leadership. Fear could demand obedience but never inspire loyalty. It could control but never truly lead. I didn't have the words for it yet, but I was beginning to see that fear and respect were not the same thing, and they create two very different outcomes.

Then came Rakim. One of my early mentors in the streets, whom I met around age fourteen. For the first time, I saw leadership differently. He wasn't the loudest, most violent, or feared, but he commanded respect because he cared about people and his crew. Before Rakim, I knew no other way to lead or get respect other than what the streets had shown me.

Rakim was from the Fort Greene section of Brooklyn, but I met him because he had family in the Tompkins Projects in Bedford-Stuyvesant, where I was from. He moved effortlessly throughout the city, respected in places where others had to prove themselves. After we met in 1993, he and I grew closer, and he would be the one to eventually give me a nickname a few years later in 1997 that stuck: "Diamond Boy." My nickname was already "D-Boy," but once I started wearing expensive diamond jewelry, which became my signature look, Rakim started calling me "Diamond Boy." The name stuck, and from that point on, that's what the inner circle called me, or Diamond for short.

Rakim wasn't the kind of guy who commanded attention with size or intimidation. In fact, he was the opposite of the muscle-bound figures who usually ruled the streets. Short, lean but solid, he wasn't someone you feared on sight, nor someone you overlooked either. There was no menace in his posture, no aggression in his eyes. He carried himself with a quiet confidence, a calm that stood out in a world where most men led with bravado and force.

What set Rakim apart was his smile, which was wide, warm, and disarming. It had the power to shift a room, making even hardened men drop their guard. More than an expression, it was a weapon he used as effectively as others used fists. In tense situations, when violence seemed near, that smile had a way of defusing things, reminding people there were other ways to command respect. He wasn't a punk, far from it, but he also wasn't the kind of gangster I'd been conditioned to admire. He didn't need threats or violence to make people listen.

Rakim's leadership wasn't about control or fear; it was about empowering you to be better, to rise above the circumstances that trapped so many of us. His leadership meant making sure everyone ate, everyone had a chance to succeed, and everyone felt valued. He was an unwavering example of purpose-driven leadership in the most unlikely of environments.

These principles and values are paramount if you want to build and sustain any business or organization for the long term. Rakim's influence didn't just keep the crew alive; it gave us hope and a sense of purpose. He was my first example of a leader showing that leadership isn't about force or intimidation; it's about wielding influence with a balance of strength and finesse, the Velvet Glove. It's the ability to lead with authority while wrapping it in respect, understanding, and genuine care. Even in hostile environments, Rakim proved this approach isn't a weakness; it's a strategy that commands lasting loyalty.

One of the first moments that made me see Rakim differently as a leader happened before we ever officially teamed up. We were still in the early stages of getting to know each other, and I was still trying to figure him out. He wasn't one who ruled with intimidation, barking orders, and expecting immediate compliance. That difference became crystal clear one day when two of his friends, Jay and Wise, got into it.

It started over something trivial, the kind of petty disagreement that normally wouldn't be worth remembering. But in the streets, small sparks could ignite something bigger. Their argument escalated fast; voices rising, tempers flaring, neither willing to back down. I had seen this scene a hundred times before, and it always ended the same. If a leader stepped in, it wasn't to mediate, it was to shut things down: "Cut that shit out," or "Shut the fuck up, we don't got time for this." Out of fear or respect, the argument would usually die. No resolution. No real conversation. Just silence imposed by authority, leaving behind resentment that silently festered.

But Rakim didn't handle it that way.

Instead of shutting them down, he stepped between them, not aggressively, not with force, but with control. He didn't bark at them to stop or flex his status. He did something I had never seen a leader in the hood do before: he listened.

He let Jay speak his piece. Then he let Wise do the same. No interruptions, no dismissiveness. Just two men being heard. When they finished, Rakim didn't pick sides or play favorites. He pointed out where each was coming from, broke it down so they could see the bigger picture, and by the end, Jay and Wise weren't just calmer, but they actually understood each other.

To me, that was mind-blowing.

I had never seen a street dispute settled like that, where feelings, perspectives, and respect were factored in and nobody walked away looking weak. Rakim didn't need to raise his voice, issue threats, or assert dominance to squash the problem. Yet his influence was just as powerful, if not more, than the fear-based leadership I had grown up with.

That was the first time I witnessed what I now call the *Velvet Glove* approach: leading not with brute force but with wisdom, patience, and the ability to make people feel seen. Back then, I wasn't fully sold. I still believed strength was measured by how much fear you could command. But that moment planted a seed. Over time, I saw the real power in Rakim's way. The kind of power that didn't just control people in the moment but earned respect that lasted.

His pure intentions and charisma carried him further than brute force ever could. Years later, I found the same approach allowed me not just to survive but to thrive. Rakim and I are both living proof of the power of leading with purpose rather than fear. We're both alive and thriving today because of it. Me on the East Coast, and him in the South as a business owner. We're still the best of friends, with plans to start a business together in Tennessee this year.

Translating Street Lessons to the Boardroom

When I transitioned to the business world, I realized that the principles of leadership I learned on the streets were just as applicable in business, perhaps even more critical. In a world where success is measured by numbers and bottom lines, it's easy to lose sight of the people who make that success possible. But the best leaders, the ones who leave a lasting impact, never forget that their primary role is to serve their people.

In any environment, a leader's power comes from the ability to inspire others to rise. It's about creating a culture where everyone feels seen, heard, and valued, where everyone has a chance to contribute and is encouraged to reach their full potential. It's about understanding that your success is tied to the success of those around you. Yet as beautiful and easy as that sounds, in company cultures across the world, this kind of leadership is often lacking, just like on the streets.

In fact, a 2023 Gallup survey reported by Denise McClain and Ryan Pendell found that 79% of lower-level management and employees report that they don't trust leadership at their respective organizations, leaving a mere 21% who say they do. That survey marked an attention-worthy decline from its 2019 peak in trust and respect. This raises a concerning reality: not just about the morale within America's workforce but also the lack of relational skills among today's leaders.

I saw this firsthand when I was hired by Gerry Butler, then CEO of a large security corporation and once named one of New York's youngest millionaires. Gerry and his leadership team were facing employee turnover of nearly 25%, and profits were stuck at a standstill quarter after quarter. They couldn't pinpoint the problem.

When my team and I walked into the company's headquarters, I could feel the tension. The atmosphere was heavy with disengagement and frustration. Employees filed into the conference room for our first meeting, their eyes showing defeat. I wasn't new to this; leadership had clearly lost touch with the people driving the company's success. Later, in one-on-one talks with staff, we learned the energy that was once vibrant and enthusiastic had fizzled out. I knew I had to understand why.

As we interviewed staff and executives, the root cause became clear: the leadership team was disconnected. Their decisions lacked purpose and intent. The focus had shifted to profits and metrics, leaving employees feeling like cogs in a machine with no room for growth or autonomy. Trust in leadership had eroded, and turnover was skyrocketing as both mid-level managers and employees fled. After countless interviews and focus groups, my team and I identified the core problem: a lack of purpose-driven leadership.

It wasn't just about numbers; it was about the lack of purpose. Leadership wasn't leading with a mission that inspired. And without empowerment, the employees had no reason to invest emotionally or mentally in their work. Turnover was a symptom of a deeper illness: a disconnection between what leadership said and what employees needed.

When I sat down with the executive team, their frustration was evident. They were hemorrhaging employees, but they couldn't pinpoint why. They had theories, of course. Assumptions dressed up as facts. But as I listened, I realized their understanding of the problem was just as shallow as the solutions they were trying to implement.

For example, when I asked them why they thought people were leaving, their responses were generic:

- "It's just the industry; turnover is high everywhere."
- "Younger employees these days don't have the same work ethic."
- "People just want more money, and we can't compete with bigger firms."

On the surface, these might seem like reasonable explanations, but they weren't answers; they were excuses. They were broad, impersonal, and placed the blame everywhere except where it belonged. The leadership team had spent so much time assuming the *what* that they had never dug into the *why.*

And that's because they weren't asking the right questions.

Instead of asking, "Why do people keep leaving?"—a question that invites assumptions—they should have been asking:

- "What specifically about our workplace makes employees disengage?"
- "What are employees telling us about their frustrations before they quit?"
- "Are managers creating an environment where people feel valued and heard?"
- "If salary isn't the main issue, what aspects of their daily experience are making them want to leave?"

But those questions were never on the table. They hadn't conducted meaningful exit interviews, tracked trends in why people left, or asked employees who stayed, "What keeps you here?" or "What almost made you leave?"

Because they hadn't asked the right questions, they were stuck with surface-level answers. Employees weren't leaving just because of salary or industry norms. They were leaving because they felt unseen. Because leadership only engaged with them when there was a problem, not as part of building a strong culture. Because promotions were based on tenure, not talent. Because managers gave orders but not feedback, and certainly not appreciation.

Once we started asking the right questions, the answers told a different story: one that was hidden in plain sight. It wasn't that people didn't want to work there. It was that leadership hadn't given them a reason to stay. They lacked purpose-driven leadership.

After an intense conversation with leadership, I outlined three core strategies that would fundamentally change the dynamic within the organization.

Strategy 1: Instilling Purpose and Transparency in Leadership.

First order of business: restore trust. Leadership needed to articulate a purpose beyond profits. Something that aligned with the company values and employees' personal goals.

We held a purpose workshop where each member of the leadership team was required to share personal stories about why they chose to lead, and how that aligned with the company's mission. These stories were then shared with the entire organization, establishing a sense of vulnerability and authenticity.

We also implemented a transparent decision-making process. Leadership committed to explaining not just *what* decisions were made but *why*. Employees had a seat at the table through regular town-hall-style meetings, where they could ask candid questions and receive straightforward answers.

Strategy 2: Empowerment Through Leadership Development.

The second strategy focused on empowering employees to lead in their own right. We developed an internal leadership program that allowed staff at all levels to participate in decision-making and problem-solving processes. Each department selected a team lead who would be trained in core leadership principles like empathy, accountability, and creative problem-solving.

These new leaders were not just chosen for their expertise but for their ability to inspire and uplift their colleagues. Leadership became less about title and more about action. With clear paths for growth and the power to contribute meaningfully, employees began to take ownership of their roles again.

Strategy 3: Fostering a Culture of Recognition and Accountability.

The third strategy focused on fostering a culture of recognition and accountability. We implemented a peer-recognition system in which employees publicly highlighted colleagues' contributions. At the same time, we held leadership accountable through quarterly evaluations from their teams.

These evaluations weren't just about metrics; they focused on whether leadership empowered employees, listened to them, and provided opportunities for growth and development. Leaders who fell short were given a chance to improve with clear feedback. If improvement was not forthcoming, further action was taken. This created mutual accountability where both leaders and employees were held to the same standard.

The Outcome

Over a year later, when I returned for a walk-through and leadership meetings, I immediately felt the difference. The energy had shifted. Once tense conversations were now open and constructive. Teams that used to avoid each other were starting to engage. Leaders kept their commitments, and the structures we'd put in place guided real connection.

The numbers told one part of the story: employee turnover had dropped from 25% to 17%, an 8-point reduction. Engagement, which had been just under 30%, had increased to about 36-37%. Yet being there in the room made it real. I could feel it in the interactions, in the laughter, and in the willingness to be accountable to one another. A few employees I'd come to know walked past with a nod or a quiet smile, the kind that said, "This place feels different. I can see myself here." It was subtle but powerful; the culture was no longer just improving on paper. It was alive.

The company was thriving, not just financially but emotionally as well. Employees could see a future for themselves, knowing their voices mattered. The transformation didn't happen overnight, but it happened because leadership finally understood that their role wasn't just to manage. It was to lead with purpose, to empower, and to connect.

Conclusion: The Lasting Legacy of Purposeful Leadership

As we close this chapter, understand that true leadership isn't anchored in titles, accolades, or control. It's rooted in empowering others; not just to follow but to rise alongside you as leaders in their own right. Purpose-driven leadership is a call to serve, to lift others even when the weight feels heavy, to put the collective good ahead of self-interest and fleeting ambition.

Through every experience, from my mother's lessons in Brooklyn to the power of respect in the streets to the boardrooms of corporate America, one thing remains clear: leadership defined by purpose, love, and empathy is the blueprint for lasting success. It not only aims for results, but also seeks to change lives, build thriving communities, and inspire others to step into their best selves.

We may not be able to choose where we begin, but we can choose how we lead. That truth holds in the toughest environments and the most established circles. Leaders who create real impact do not simply wield authority. They equip others with the tools, confidence, and wisdom to lead alongside them.

With purpose-driven leadership, you don't just make progress; you help others make progress with you, building a vision bigger than yourself with every decision, every encounter, and every challenge you face.

As you reflect on the lessons shared in these pages, know that the power to lead with purpose is within you. It starts with understanding this enduring truth: leadership without purpose is fleeting, but leadership with purpose has the power to shape lives, transform organizations, and change the world. Make your legacy one that uplifts, empowers, and inspires—leaving a lasting imprint on all those fortunate enough to walk with you.

Actionable Steps for Purpose-Driven Leadership

1. **Put People First:** Prioritize the needs and growth of your team members. Invest in their development, provide opportunities for advancement, and create a supportive and empowering environment. Remember, your role as a leader is to serve, not to be served.

   Example: Imagine leading a team during a company-wide downsizing. Instead of focusing solely on cutting costs, you take the time to understand each team member's individual needs, offering personalized support such as connecting them with career services or internal opportunities. By doing this, you show that the company values people over numbers, increasing trust and loyalty even in difficult times.

2. **Lead by Example:** Demonstrate the behaviors you expect from your team. Show compassion, integrity, and a genuine commitment to their success. Be the first to lend a hand, the first to acknowledge a mistake, and the first to celebrate a win.

   Example: As a department head, a mistake causes a client to lose faith. Instead of blaming the team, you acknowledge your role and work to fix the issue, showing accountability. This strengthens trust and fosters a culture of openness and integrity.

3. **Recognize and Reward:** Acknowledge the contributions of your team members, both individually and collectively. Celebrate their successes and show appreciation for their hard work. Recognition doesn't have to be monetary;

often, a simple acknowledgment of their efforts can have a profound impact.

Example: Say you are a leader of a tech company, where innovation is critical. You initiate a "Recognition Friday," where every team member can publicly acknowledge another's contribution for the week, be it a small or large achievement. Even without monetary rewards, this practice boosts morale and promotes a culture of appreciation.

4. **Foster a Culture of Empowerment:** Encourage your team to take ownership of their work, make decisions, and contribute ideas. Create a safe space for open communication and feedback, so they know that their voice matters and that their contributions are valued.

   Example: As a startup founder, you give your junior employees the freedom to lead projects, make decisions, and their ideas directly to leadership. This encourages breakthroughs, as employees feel a sense of ownership over their work and are encouraged to think outside the box, knowing they are trusted and respected for their contributions.

5. **Focus on the Greater Good:** Align your leadership with a higher purpose, whether it's serving your community, improving the environment, or making a positive impact on the world. When your team knows their work is contributing to something bigger than themselves, they'll be more motivated and engaged. If you were the head of a

socially responsible company, you would align business goals with community service.

Example: You offer employees paid time off to volunteer at local charities. This demonstrates that your organization values impact beyond profit, which can drive employee engagement and retention as well as be the difference your client is looking for in a company they want to do business with.

Leadership Reflection

1. In what ways might you currently be leading through fear, control, title, or authority instead of trust, empowerment, and purpose? What steps will you take to change that?

2. Think about a leader, mentor, parent, coach, or colleague who impacted your life in a positive way. What specific qualities made their leadership meaningful and lasting?

List up to 3 ways you can empower others through your leadership.

1.

2.

3.

I have not failed. I've just found 10,000 ways that won't work.

—Thomas Edison

CHAPTER 2

EMBRACE FAILURE — LEARN AND GROW FROM SETBACKS

Failure as the Foundation of Leadership

IN LEADERSHIP, TRUE strength isn't measured by flawless victories but by the courage to embrace failure as a stepping stone to greatness. This chapter invites you into the hardships where setbacks become wisdom and humiliation becomes resilience. Here, we dismantle the myth that success is a straight path, revealing instead that every stumble, every moment of despair, and every raw, unfiltered defeat is a powerful teacher.

From the unforgiving streets to the rigid discipline of boot camp, from entrepreneurship to my darkest moments of vulnerability, failure has been my most honest mentor. It stripped away illusions, exposed limitations, and, most importantly, honed the humility, empathy, and emotional intelligence essential for leadership.

Prepare to embark on a journey where every scar is a badge of honor, a symbol of growth, a testament to the power of resilience, and a reminder that the road to success is paved with the lessons of our most profound setbacks. Welcome to the transformative power of embracing failure. It is within these moments of vulnerability that your true leadership potential is forged.

The Role of Failure in Leadership

My experiences taught me a fundamental truth: leadership isn't about avoiding failure but embracing it as a catalyst for growth. Failure forges the best leaders through learning and the continual development of the human side of leadership: humility, empathy, and emotional intelligence.

My path has been marked by both triumphs and setbacks, yet each misstep and each failed initiative has been an invaluable teacher. Failure sharpened my leadership skills and strengthened my resilience.

Failure is often seen as something to fear or avoid. In reality, it is one of life's most powerful teachers. We rarely grow during times of comfort or success. Growth happens when we are forced to confront our limitations, question our assumptions, and close the gaps in our knowledge. Failure demands self-awareness. It forces us to examine our decisions, understand our emotions, and lead with greater clarity and intention.

The Tennessee Debacle: A Humbling Setback

One of the most humbling lessons of my life came at just fourteen years old, during my earliest brush with the drug trade. I was young, reckless, and hungry for success, too full of myself to realize how unprepared I truly was. Desperate to prove my worth, not just to myself but to Rakim and his team, I agreed to a mission far beyond my experience: a solo trip to Tennessee in 1994.

At the time, I had never sold drugs, never left New York except with family, and certainly had no ties to Tennessee. But Rakim's friend, Wise, had spent time there and had loose connections. After suffering a major financial loss in Utica, NY, Rakim and his team saw an opportunity to rebuild in Johnson City, Tennessee, and my fearless, naive ambition made me eager for the first trip. They sent me with a small package of drugs, trusting that I'd figure it out.

I left home without telling a soul, trusting only my brother Jason with this information, driven by fantasies of fast money, the kind I had seen in movies. My only contact was an older woman Wise had once known, who was supposed to provide a place to stay. That was the extent of my plan. No experience. No real understanding of the market. No backup if things went wrong.

Failure was inevitable. And it came swiftly.

The streets of Tennessee were nothing like Brooklyn. The energy, the people, and even the rules of the game were all different. Back home, the hustle never stopped. But in Johnson City, the pace was slower, quieter. What I didn't realize was that beneath that calm surface lurked a world I wasn't prepared for: undercover cops, snitches, informants, and a cutthroat mentality where survival meant selling out whoever it took. In Brooklyn, that kind of betrayal was unheard of because the consequences were too dire. So, it never crossed my young mind. I had no idea what I had just walked into.

Still, I got to work, moving what I had. But I was a kid playing a grown man's game, and it showed. No one had taught me the first thing about money, how to manage it, or how to make it last. I spent without thinking, not understanding that the "re-up" money, the cash needed to restock, was untouchable. Malls, restaurants, reckless spending, it all added up. Before I knew it, I was tapped out.

Broke and out of product, my problems stacked up fast. The woman I was staying with had no use for a kid who couldn't contribute, and before long, I was on the street. Just like that, I was homeless. No money, no connections, and no way back to New York.

I slept in hallways, parks, or wherever I could. I stole food just to get by. But the lowest point came one night when hunger hit harder than ever. Desperate, I found myself digging through the trash behind a restaurant, knowing they threw food away at closing time. The humiliation burned deep. I had left home chasing an illusion of power and success, and here I was, scavenging like an animal.

That moment, as I kneeled by that back door, near the dumpster, with tears streaming down my face, was both deeply humiliating and humbling. My frail fourteen-year-old body fought against the chill of the night, but the cold was nothing compared to the harsh realization settling in. It was a first-class lesson in how overconfidence and poor planning had led me here, to this moment of regret and vulnerability. A lesson I would never forget, yet it would not be my last.

In the years that followed, the streets continued to teach me harsh lessons about leadership and decision-making. I suffered financial catastrophes, including losses of over half a million dollars due to misreading politics and street dynamics. Violence took friends from me, losses that were irreplaceable. I faced near-death experiences more than once in the brutal world of street culture.

But those losses became knowledge and wisdom, shaping my ability to navigate almost any arena in life.

It wasn't just my pride that took a hit; these experiences reshaped me. They taught me empathy in ways nothing else could. Struggling with vulnerability, I began to see the world differently. I learned to read people, sense their unspoken burdens, and navigate different cultures and backgrounds.

Failure humbled me, but it also revealed a deeper truth: we all fall at some point. And when you've felt the pain of falling, you gain the power to help others rise. Leadership isn't about standing tall alone; it's about reaching back, lifting others, and making sure no one is left behind.

Failure sharpened my emotional intelligence. It strengthened my ability to recognize, understand, and manage my own emotions while navigating the emotions of others. This skill is critical in moments of fear and desperation, when survival depends on accurately reading people and situations.

Some of my hardest lessons came in the streets. Losses taught me quickly that desperation changes people. Hunger, fear, and uncertainty can turn friends into enemies and break even the strongest. But instead of letting bitterness consume me, I paid attention, not just to what people said but to what they didn't. I learned to read body language, shifts in tone, and the hesitation before a lie. I recognized the masks people wore to hide their struggles because I wore one too.

Emotional intelligence isn't just about understanding others; it's about managing yourself in crisis. I learned to control my impulses, stay calm in chaos, and respond rather than react. That awareness became one of my greatest assets, not just for surviving but for leading. True leadership isn't only about decisions; it's about understanding the hearts and minds of those you lead when the stakes are high.

I could have let anger or frustration rule me, but instead, I channeled those emotions into determination. Through these experiences, I learned that a leader's ability to manage emotions in the face of failure is one of their greatest strengths.

A Second Chance: Learning from Failure

One afternoon in Johnson City, being homeless, starving, and desperate, I stole a juice and a sandwich from a gas station. As I walked out, an older white woman caught my eye. She had seen everything. I braced myself for anger or the police, but instead, her eyes showed something different: concern.

She approached, not with accusation but with quiet curiosity. "Why are you stealing?" she asked.

I almost lashed out, ready to tell her to mind her business. But something about her was warm and disarming. In that moment of shame and exhaustion, I let my guard down. I told her everything: how I had lost everything, had no way home, and was surviving off scraps.

She listened. Then, to my surprise, she told me to get in her car.

I hesitated. I didn't know her. I had no reason to trust her. But something told me to go. We drove in silence to a small church. Inside, she introduced me to a group of people, then disappeared to the back of the church. When she returned, she told me they were buying me a one-way ticket back to New York. I would stay there for a day or two, then finally go home.

I never saw her again. I cannot remember her name. But I have never forgotten her kindness.

When I returned to Brooklyn, I felt defeated but not broken. Rakim didn't chastise me or treat me like a lost cause. Instead, he saw something I couldn't yet see in myself. He acknowledged the lessons I had learned, the growth that had resulted from my mistakes. Failure hadn't crushed me; it had humbled me, shaped me, and made me more determined.

That experience taught me something invaluable about leadership. True leaders don't just measure people by their successes; they see the potential in their failures. They recognize growth even when it's wrapped in struggle. And sometimes, the smallest act of kindness, like a stranger offering a way home, can change everything.

Yet Rakim also acknowledged his own mistakes and his failure to properly prepare me for the experience, something you seldom, if ever, see leaders in the streets do. That in itself was a powerful lesson for me: to see a leader take ownership of his part of the failure. It was empowering to see that quality as a strength and not a weakness. I would later use these qualities to not only build a million-dollar drug operation but also, years after my fall, to build a million-dollar business portfolio and help other people do the same.

This second chance to return to Tennessee with Rakim was pivotal. His empathy helped me see that true leaders don't just tolerate failure; they embrace it as a stepping stone to wisdom. He didn't see my failure as the end but as education, making me sharper, more aware, and a stronger leader. And he wasn't the only one learning. His response taught me a crucial lesson: great leaders don't discard people when they fall; they use those moments to build them up.

With that mindset, I approached my second trip to Tennessee differently. Though I lost money and drugs on the first run, my time hadn't been wasted. I had studied the city, its layout, players, and street politics. I mapped movements, alliances, and unspoken rules that governed Johnson City. That knowledge proved more valuable than the product I lost. By the time I returned, I knew the city and surrounding towns like the back of my hand, and this time, I wasn't going alone.

Rakim and the team came with me. This wasn't just about hustling; it was about strategy. We weren't just carrying drugs this time; we carried insight, experience, and a plan. I had learned from mistakes, grown more emotionally aware, and understood the importance of calculated moves over reckless ambition.

But Tennessee still had more lessons to teach me. This second trip, though a little longer than my prior four-month stay and more successful in terms of money made and length of time there, would ultimately lead to my downfall. The same streets I had studied so carefully became the ones that trapped me. The game I thought I had figured out had rules I hadn't yet learned. This time, my run ended in handcuffs, facing drug charges that would send me to a juvenile detention center in Tennessee in 1994, then to the adolescent prison called Mountain View, where I would ultimately be held until the summer of 1995.

By the summer of '95, I walked out of Mountain View a changed person, but not reformed. I was harder, smarter, and more focused. Over the next few years, I rebuilt the hustle, this time with strategy and scars. By 1998, I wasn't just in the game; I was running it.

Looking back, that experience didn't just teach me the cost of failure; it taught me the weight of leadership. Knowledge without wisdom is dangerous. Confidence without discipline is reckless. And failure, no matter how painful, is often the foundation of growth.

Military Boot Camp: Failure as a Pathway to Resilience

A few years after my 1994 experience in Tennessee, by 1998, at about nineteen, I had become a well-established dealer, running a growing enterprise with confidence and precision. Business was booming, and I had built a network that stretched across state lines, from Massachusetts, New York, back to Tennessee, and then to Maryland in 1999. But with success came risk, and one fateful trip to New York would change the course of my life forever.

That day, I wasn't alone. A woman came with me to pick up a large supply of drugs, simple and routine, or so I thought. But things took a sharp turn when narcotics police caught her. I wasn't even on the scene, just nearby, yet they arrested me, too. The moment the cuffs locked, something felt off. It seemed orchestrated, like a setup. Never proven, maybe just paranoia.

Facing serious charges, I hired the best legal defense money could buy. My attorneys maneuvered through the system and negotiated a deal that changed my life. Instead of the high-level offense that could have buried me, they reduced it significantly. Then came the game-changing option: because it was my first adult offense, I was given a choice: prison or a seven-month military-style program.

The choice was clear. I chose the academy, not out of a sudden embrace of patriotism, but because the streets had taught me to weigh options carefully, and the alternative, returning to a life of confinement and prison, wasn't one I'd take. I had no interest in trading my freedom for a cell, even if it meant stepping into what I jokingly called "the world of G.I. Joe." But I had no idea what I was walking into. I had survived the streets, navigated danger, and built a street empire, but nothing could have prepared me for the rigid discipline and relentless structure of military-style living.

By 1999, the date was set for me to report to Moriah Boot Camp Academy. My path was no longer mine to control. The streets had taught me how to move, but now I was about to learn an entirely different way of life. One that would test me in ways I never imagined.

The lessons of failure followed me beyond the streets of Tennessee and into my time at this military program. Military-style life was structured, disciplined, and full of challenges. But failure was ever-present. Whether it was messing up a drill, missing a target, or failing a physical test, we were constantly pushed to our limits. Unlike in the streets, failure here was an expected part of the growth process.

The program taught me perseverance and resilience. It's where I learned to respect the chain of command, a lesson valuable later in life. Military life tested both mind and body, pushing us to build both.

From the moment I arrived at Moriah, drill instructors were watching. Unknown to me, they were already searching for leadership potential, evaluating how we moved, responded under pressure, and interacted. Their goal: find five individuals, four squad leaders, and one platoon leader, who could bring order to the chaos.

Our platoon, the "Wolf Pack," was exactly what instructors expected: unorganized, out of sync, and struggling. But as days went on, they watched closely. In training, they saw who took initiative. On runs, they saw who lagged and who went back to help. Without aiming for rank, I found myself stepping in: running beside stragglers, encouraging, and guiding during drills. I wasn't angling for a position; I didn't even know such roles existed. It was just who I was. In the streets, my philosophy was simple: put your team first. For the next seven months, these men were my team.

It wasn't long before the drill instructors took notice. Two weeks into the program, I was called forward and officially named platoon leader, a sixty-man unit for which I was now responsible. At that moment, I had no idea how profound this role would be or the doors it would open for me. What I saw as a simple responsibility turned out to be an opportunity of a lifetime.

In this position, I gained unprecedented access to some of the most decorated and battle-tested leaders in the military: Marines, Army officers, and Navy SEALs—men whose leadership had been forged in real-world combat. At just nineteen years old, I had the privilege of being mentored by some of the greatest minds in leadership. They didn't just teach me about authority; they showed me what it truly meant to lead, not through fear or force, but through example, discipline, and an unwavering commitment to those under my charge.

What I learned in those months changed the way I saw leadership forever.

My platoon was overseen by three drill instructors: DI Morehouse, DI Wolf, and DI Blaze. All were strong leaders but with very different styles. DI Wolf wasn't afraid to cry when the situation called for it, demonstrating to me the power of vulnerability in leadership. DI Morehouse was "no joke" but had a hidden, softer side; he never attended graduations because goodbyes were hard. DI Blaze was hardcore and strictly business, keeping us sharp and on our toes whenever he was around. Fortunately, he took a personal liking to me.

Together, they were a perfect blend; proof that there's no one-size-fits-all approach to leadership. Each complemented the others, creating a balanced training experience that prepared us for real-world complexity. While different in approach, they shared the same commitment and goal.

Observing these leaders in action, I realized that effective leadership is fluid, adaptable, and requires a diverse set of tools. At times, empathy and understanding are needed to connect with and motivate individuals. Other times, a firm hand and clear expectations are necessary to maintain order and achieve goals. And in critical moments, unwavering resolve and a no-nonsense attitude can make all the difference. A blend of all three is what I aspired to be, and, ultimately, became as a leader. I'm thankful for all I learned in that experience, from them and the other leaders there.

When I did fail at certain things, like an obstacle course, or made a decision that didn't work for the platoon, DI Morehouse would pull me aside and say, "Failure's not about how many times you fall down. It's about how many times you get back up and push forward."

This lesson wasn't just about the obstacle course; it was about life. The road to success is not easy and not paved with flowers. Life is going to test you to see how badly you want it, and unfortunately, loss and failure are part of the process. He helped me understand that failure was not the opposite or absence of success but a part of success, a necessary by-product.

The program showed me that failure builds resilience, and resilience builds leadership. The humility to accept failure, empathy to know everyone fails, and emotional intelligence to manage it all. These are the true keys to thriving in hard situations.

Failure in the Business World: A Different Kind of Setback

In my early twenties, around 2001, I had a bold vision: to open several clothing stores in three different malls. At the time, I was still deep in the drug game, but I had begun thinking about my future beyond the streets. I knew I couldn't do this forever; I needed an exit plan. This venture into retail was my first real attempt at legitimate business and entrepreneurship.

I had a few connections who could get me into certain malls, and with money in my pocket, I figured I had everything I needed to succeed. But there was one glaring problem: I had no idea what I was doing. I had no real knowledge of the retail market, how it worked, or what it took to scale a business. I assumed that if I had a good product and the money to invest, everything else would fall into place.

But business doesn't work like that. For example, I didn't understand inventory management. I bought what I thought looked good, not what the market demanded.

- I didn't analyze consumer trends or study foot-traffic patterns in the malls I was in.
- I had no pricing strategy beyond guessing what felt reasonable.
- I thought high-end fashion items would automatically attract customers, but I failed to consider seasonal trends, proper branding, or positioning against competitors.

On top of that, I made uninformed decisions and overestimated my capabilities. One prime example was my approach to hiring: instead of bringing in experienced retail managers, I relied on people I trusted from my old life, friends who, like me, had no business experience. I assumed loyalty would translate into competency, but it didn't. Employees mishandled inventory, customer service was inconsistent, and there was little to no real structure in place to keep things running smoothly.

To make matters worse, I signed multiple expensive leases without fully understanding the financial risks, assuming my initial investment would carry me through. I underestimated operating costs, rent, payroll, marketing, and inventory restocking, and before I knew it, expenses were piling up faster than revenue was coming in.

Ultimately, I lost more money than I care to admit. The stores never reached their potential, and everything fell apart. It was a hard lesson but a necessary one. Looking back, I see that I wasn't just trying to build a business; I was trying to escape my past without fully preparing for my future. And in business, as in life, preparation is everything.

I could have given up, but I'm not the "give up" type. I would fail other times and in other aspects of life, but each of these failures was a lesson in humility. I had to stop and be present and ask myself, "What am I missing?"

The answer came years later—when I gave another go at entrepreneurial life in 2020—this time laying the groundwork and blueprint for Motivational Dreamers and my real estate company. This time, I understood the importance of mentorship, investing in yourself, and becoming well-versed in your field. I learned to trust my instincts, surround myself with people who balanced my weaknesses, and clarify my purpose and gifts. Most importantly, I wasn't just winging a business because it "felt" right anymore.

It was in that moment of clarity, reflecting on failure, understanding my values, and recognizing my purpose, that I was ready to move into the next phase of my journey.

These values, which I learned through what most would call failure, gave birth to my role as CEO and founder of Motivational Dreamers Inc., a successful national consulting and professional speaking business. They led to the formation of the TEARS Organization, the philanthropic arm of my portfolio, which has since been fully integrated into Motivational Dreamers, and the co-founding of the No Longer 3/5th Coalition, a coalition of individual activists and organizations. Under the leadership of Derrick Washington and myself, the coalition is doing phenomenal work statewide in Massachusetts. This journey also led to the creation of DKB Estates, the real estate arm of my businesses operating in South Carolina and Massachusetts.

Let's be very clear: building these organizations, companies, and the vast network it took to sustain them did not happen by chance or mistake. Nor did it happen overnight. It took careful planning, patience, and humility. The foundation for these endeavors was laid long before I left prison, but the real education began the moment I was released.

I had studied business books while incarcerated, but no amount of reading could prepare me for the lessons that came from being in the trenches, navigating the real world in real time. I made a crucial decision upon my release: instead of returning to New York, where old habits and familiar faces could pull me backward, I chose Boston, a city I had never been to. I wanted a fresh start, a new perspective on life, and the chance to rebuild without the weight of my past surroundings.

From day one, I got to work. I knew what I wanted: to build a legacy my family would be proud of, and more importantly, I knew what I needed. I worked multiple jobs, building capital to add to the money I had already saved. Beyond the financial aspect, I quickly realized that I had returned to a world that was nothing like the one I had left behind nineteen years prior.

When I went to prison, smartphones didn't exist. There was no instant access to information at your fingertips, no social media connecting people across industries in seconds. I remember coming home, seeing this new digital landscape, and thinking, *How isn't everyone winning out here?* For those of us old enough to remember, I come from the era of libraries and the Dewey Decimal System, where you could spend almost a whole day searching for a single piece of information. Now, with the touch of a button, unlimited information was available instantly. I found that truly amazing.

Even while working long hours, I used every spare moment for research. I went to community events nonstop, determined to meet the right people, networking as if my life depended on it because, in many ways, it did. I leveraged social media to find key gatherings across the country, traveling to attend, shaking hands, and building relationships. That relentless push expanded my network nationally, and soon I was known not just in Boston's social, civic, and political spaces, but across Massachusetts. That credibility led to co-founding the No Longer 3/5ths Coalition, cementing my place in civic advocacy and leadership.

In late 2021, I established Motivational Dreamers, which launched me into an entirely new phase of learning. I asked myself a pivotal question: "What does it truly mean to be a CEO and run a company?" I knew I had leadership skills, but I also knew the smartest path forward was to seek out mentors, people who had already walked the path I was stepping onto. I scheduled countless meetings, both in person and over Zoom. Sitting down with CEOs, founders, and business leaders, soaking up their wisdom.

That decision to humble myself and learn from those who had already succeeded made all the difference. They didn't just teach me the mechanics of running a company; they saved me from countless mistakes and unnecessary failures. I also learned from many of them the importance of embracing failure as part of the process, a common theme among every true and successful leader I've ever met.

This was the true beginning of building legitimate businesses and stepping fully into entrepreneurship. Over time, I would go on to share space and stages with some of the biggest names in the speaking world, corporate sector, politics, grassroots movements, and real estate. With each opportunity, my expertise grew, and eventually, I became a sought-after authority in these fields.

What set me apart wasn't just my ability to lead but the depth of my leadership experience across vastly different arenas. Having navigated high-stakes environments all my life, from the streets and prison to boardrooms, advocacy circles, and corporate and nonprofit consulting—I gained an edge. I saw gray areas and blind spots others missed, and that ability became my greatest strength.

My experiences taught me that creating a culture that accepts failure is crucial for innovation. When people are afraid to fail, they avoid risks. Hesitation kills creativity. But when failure is seen as a teacher, teams become more innovative, resilient, and adaptable.

Conclusion: Rising Strong from Every Setback

Failure is not your enemy; it is the fashion in which you are shaped into a leader. Every hardship and setback is not a sign of weakness but a lesson in resilience, humility, and growth. It's through the moments of failure that I found my highest calling: by embracing it, learning from it, and using it to push forward with unshakable confidence.

In the streets, in prison, and in business, I was no stranger to failure. Whether it was losing everything in Tennessee, navigating hard lessons through incarceration, picking myself up after a catastrophic business venture, or learning to lead through adversity, every failure taught me something invaluable. Beyond the lessons on smarter decisions, true leadership was forged in the fires of failure.

It's not the wounds that define us but how we rise from them. The real power of failure isn't in its ability to drag you down but in its charge to build a stronger, wiser version of yourself. Failure is a springboard, launching you further than you ever thought possible. The key lies not in avoiding failure but in using it as a tool for progress.

However, embracing failure doesn't mean tolerating complacency. To create a culture where failure is truly a stepping stone rather than a stumbling block, every setback must be met with reflection, adaptation, and improvement. Failure only serves its purpose if we extract the lessons it offers and refuse to repeat the same mistakes.

As a leader, your role is not to shield your team from falling but to guide them when they do. In those moments, the most significant transformations happen. True leadership is revealed in how you respond to failure—how you rise, adapt, and move forward with renewed purpose.

Actionable Steps for Leaders to Embrace Failure

1. **Reframe Failure:** See failure not as a personal shortcoming but as a learning opportunity. Emphasize that it's part of the journey, not the end. Share this perspective so your team views setbacks more positively.

   Example: Imagine you are launching a new product line at a tech company that doesn't meet customer expectations. Instead of seeing it as a loss, gather the team to analyze customer feedback and sales data. Use these insights to refine the product and create a more successful iteration. By reframing failure, your team learns that setbacks are opportunities for improvement, not defeats.

2. **Analyze Your Mistakes:** Take the time to reflect on your setbacks. Ask yourself, "What went wrong? Why did it happen? What could I have done differently?" The more you dissect your failures, the more you'll learn from them. This reflective process is crucial for developing better strategies and improving decision-making.

   Example: After his company lost three significant clients, I was hired by CEO Jerry Bass. I met with all the leaders first, then held a team meeting to break down the reasons behind the loss, examining the preparation process, communication with the client, and the pitch strategy. Through this reflective process, my team identified areas for improvement, ensuring future pitches are stronger and more aligned with client needs.

3. **Cultivate a Growth Mindset:** In all spaces I lead, I'm a champion of adopting a growth mindset, which means embracing challenges, seeking out feedback, and viewing every experience as a chance to learn and improve. A growth mindset is about seeing potential in every setback and using it as fuel for personal and professional development.

   Example: Ask your department heads to regularly seek feedback, not just after failures but even after successes. This encourages the team to see every project as a learning opportunity. It builds a culture where employees are always seeking to improve and aren't afraid to take on challenges, knowing that growth is the ultimate goal.

4. **Create a Safe Space for Failure:** Foster an environment where your team feels comfortable taking risks and experimenting, knowing that mistakes are part of the learning process. Encourage experimentation, and when things don't go as planned, turn the conversation toward learning and growth rather than assigning blame.

   Example: At a startup, the leadership team introduces a "Fail Fast, Learn Fast" initiative. Team members are encouraged to experiment with new ideas, even if they might fail. After a marketing campaign doesn't yield results, the team doesn't assign blame; instead, they focus on what can be learned and applied to the next campaign.

5. **Lead with Openness:** Share your own experiences with failure and demonstrate how you've used those setbacks to grow and develop as a leader. By being open about your own failures, you'll not only show vulnerability but also build trust and authenticity with your team.

   Example: A CEO openly shares a story of a failed business venture during a company-wide meeting. I've done this countless times. We outline how that failure led to valuable lessons that have shaped the company's current success. Through vulnerability, the CEO builds trust and encourages team members to embrace their own failures as opportunities for growth.

6. **Reward Risk-Taking:** If your team is taking calculated risks and learning from failure, reward that effort. Recognize that the willingness to push boundaries and try new things is what drives innovation, even if the outcome isn't always successful.

   Example: A creative agency introduces a "Bold Moves" award to recognize employees who take risks, even when the outcome isn't successful. By celebrating risk-takers, the company fosters an environment where innovation thrives, and employees aren't afraid to push boundaries.

Leadership Reflection

1. How has adversity shaped the way you lead, make decisions, or respond to challenges today?

2. What is one setback in your life that helped shape your growth?

List up to three lessons you learned from failure.

1.

2.

3.

The single biggest problem in communication is the illusion that it has taken place.

—George Bernard Shaw

CHAPTER 3

MASTER THE ART OF COMMUNICATION — BUILD TRUST AND INSPIRE ACTION

The Unspoken Force of Leadership

IN EVERY MOMENT of our lives, there exists a language more profound than words. It shows up in the hushed intensity of a prison yard and the dynamic energy of a corporate room. It is woven from silent glances, measured pauses, and the raw power of presence. In this chapter, we explore the art of communication and reveal how true leaders harness not only spoken words, but also the unspoken cues that build trust, bridge divides, and inspire decisive action.

Here, you will journey through the many tests of life, where communication became a lifeline, a vital tool forged in the heat of adversity, whether on the unforgiving streets, within the confining walls of incarceration, or amid the high-stakes challenges of building a business empire. As you turn these pages, prepare to discover how every nod, every silence, and every carefully chosen word is not merely a method of expression but a powerful testament to the strength of human connection. This is the transformative power of communication: a force that can reshape destinies, ignite collective purpose, and elevate leadership to its highest calling.

Communication is the foundation upon which trust, relationships, and leadership are built. It's more than just the exchange of words; it's the exchange of understanding, the conveyance of intent, and the conduit that connects people from different walks of life. My journey in the streets, through a military program, and eventually through various stages of incarceration and into the world of corporate America, taught me that mastering the art of communication isn't just a skill; it's a lifeline.

Whatever the environment, the way you communicate can determine the difference between success and failure, between life and death. But words alone aren't enough. As I discovered in some of the most intense environments, communication goes far beyond the verbal; it also encompasses everything we don't say: the look in our eyes, the way we stand, the tone of our voice, and the energy we bring to a conversation. In the high-stakes world of leadership, these nonverbal cues can make or break relationships.

The Early Lessons: A First Taste of Confinement

As I mentioned in the last chapter, my second trip to Tennessee ended with me in handcuffs, the result of a drug bust orchestrated by a man who was supposed to be a trusted friend of Wise, someone from Johnson City, Tennessee. The clang of the cell door at Mountain View Correctional Facility echoed through my body, each reverberation hammering home the reality of my situation. This wasn't just another misstep; I had walked straight into a disaster I didn't see coming.

At just fifteen years old, I found myself incarcerated for the first time, a consequence of my choices, my lack of experience in the drug trade, and my misplaced trust. The streets had given me a sense of power, of control, but all of that was an illusion. The moment those bars slammed shut, the bravado disappeared, and I was left with nothing but cold steel and silence.

Despite being proud that I never gave anyone up to the authorities, the truth was that no one could come to my rescue. Not my mother. Not my crew. No one. The walls closed in, and for the first time, I understood I was on my own.

This wasn't prison in the way most people imagine it, no hardened criminals serving decades for violent crimes. But it was still a place where the freedom of movement, the spontaneity of life, and the basic sense of safety were stripped away. The adolescent correctional facility was a far cry from the bustling streets of Brooklyn or the quieter corners of Johnson City, Tennessee, where I had been arrested. The rigid structure, constant surveillance, and loss of freedom were a shock to my system. The swagger I had carried with me on the outside was useless here; I was just another incarcerated young man, stripped of my identity and forced to confront the consequences of my actions.

In the isolation of my cell, I wrestled with a maelstrom of emotions: nervousness, anger, betrayal, confusion, sadness, and a profound sense of loss. The streets had been my classroom, but now I was trapped in a different kind of school, one where the lessons were harsh and the curriculum was unforgiving. I was surrounded by kids just like me, young, angry, misguided, and lost. Many were already entrenched in gang life, living by a code that demanded loyalty to the point of self-destruction. I wasn't in a gang, but the pressure to choose a side was relentless.

Every day was a balancing act, navigating the tensions between different groups like the Bloods, Crips, Gangsta Disciples, and Vice Lords. I would ultimately befriend and learn from all these groups. This was my first dealings with organized street structures, but it would not be my last, unbeknownst to me at the time.

The Struggle to Communicate: More than Words

In an environment like Mountain View, communication is a minefield. Every word, every gesture could be misinterpreted, leading to conflicts that escalated faster than you could blink. I quickly learned that what you said was only part of the equation; how you said it mattered just as much, if not more. In an environment where respect was everything, nonverbal cues, the way you held yourself, your eye contact, and even your posture, could communicate more than words ever could.

In those tense environments such as the streets, I learned to read people quickly, to gauge their moods and intentions before I even opened my mouth. Your body language spoke volumes before you ever said a word. Stand too tall, and you might be seen as trying to dominate. Avoid eye contact, and you could be perceived as weak or untrustworthy. It was a delicate balance, and getting it wrong could result in dangerous misunderstandings.

But perhaps the most important lesson I learned was the power of silence. In the streets, I had been loud, brash, always quick with a comeback, always ready to prove a point. But in lockup, I realized that sometimes, the smartest move wasn't to speak, but to say nothing at all. Silence became my shield, a form of self-preservation. It kept me out of unnecessary conflicts, away from the traps of gossip, and, most importantly, it allowed me to observe and learn.

In that environment, words could be weapons or weaknesses. A simple complaint about the food could be taken as soft. A casual joke could offend the wrong person. Even asking too many questions could make you seem suspicious, like you were fishing for information. And in a place where information could get you hurt, or worse, staying quiet was often the safest choice.

I saw other people pay the price for talking too much. One guy, fresh in, started venting about his case to the wrong person, hoping to gain sympathy. A few days later, word spread that he was snitching, even though he wasn't. It didn't matter. His own words put a target on his back. Another time, I watched as two kids my age got into it over something minor; one had borrowed food and taken too long to pay it back. A third guy, thinking he was being helpful, jumped in to play peacemaker. A day later, he was jumped in the recreation area. Not because he owed anything, not because he was wrong, but because he spoke on business that wasn't his. This taught me a lesson I carry into boardrooms: speak only when the moment demands it. Silence is never neutral; it's either a strategy or surrender.

You learn quickly that silence is not just about avoiding trouble. It is a language of its own. A nod can signal respect. A blank expression can keep you neutral. A hard stare can end or start a confrontation, depending on the situation. The ones who lasted the longest, who moved through that world without making unnecessary enemies, were not the ones who talked the most. They were the ones who knew when to listen, when to observe, and when to walk away.

There's a reason that the old heads in real prison don't waste words. They understand the power of presence. Something many young men in Mountain View hadn't quite learned yet, and why there was so much conflict. I remember one older kid at Mountain View who was from Chattanooga and was eighteen years old, the oldest you can be at this facility. He barely spoke but was respected by everyone. He never raised his voice, never got involved in drama, but when he did speak, people listened. His silence made his words carry more weight. It was a reminder that in certain environments, your presence and your energy speak louder than anything you could ever say.

That was the hardest lesson to learn, not just *when* to talk, but when *not* to. Because in prison, whether juvenile or adult, and in life, sometimes the most powerful statement you can make is saying nothing at all.

Building Trust Through Nonverbal Communication

In those environments, trust wasn't always earned by what you said; many times, it was built by what you didn't say. It showed in how you carried yourself, the consistency of your actions, and the energy you projected. I learned early on that my facial expressions, tone of voice, and even my posture shaped how others perceived me.

If your words didn't align with your body language or tone, people questioned your intentions. That's true in any leadership setting, whether in business, on the streets, or in a jail yard. Authentic communication means your message and your nonverbal cues are in sync. That's how real trust is built.

Leaders who say one thing but convey something else through their tone or body language lose credibility fast. If your words don't align with your actions, you risk undermining the very trust you're trying to build. One of the truest lessons I've learned about leadership, no matter what environment, is that a title only buys you time to either increase your influence or undermine it.

Learning from Others: The Value of Listening

Another one of the most valuable lessons I learned in the streets and during my time in detention was the importance of listening. Communication isn't just about talking; it's about understanding. And understanding begins with listening. In the confines of the detention facility, I was surrounded by stories—stories of pain, of loss, of dreams deferred. Each incarcerated young man had a unique story, a journey that had led them to this place. By listening actively and empathetically, I gained insight into their motivations, fears, and dreams. These insights helped me connect with them on a deeper level, build trust, loyalty, and foster a sense of community within the detention walls.

I listened to the other young men as they recounted their experiences, both in the streets and in the system. By doing so, I gained valuable information that I could utilize in navigating the social structure within the walls of the adolescent detention center.

These skills are just as vital to me today in the business world. Knowing what makes others tick and what is important to them is invaluable. It allows me to choose my words carefully, but it also helps me recognize how nonverbal cues, such as a nod, a glance, or even a pause, can convey respect, understanding, or solidarity. Listening deeply translates into any leadership position because it helps you genuinely connect with your employees, develop trust, and respect. It is from that place that motivation and loyalty naturally rise.

The Next Chapter: The Real Education Begins

After nearly a year in Mountain View, I returned to my mother's home in Brooklyn, New York. The year was 1995. Shortly thereafter, I left New York again and joined Rakim, this time in Massachusetts. I was still searching for purpose, identity, and meaning, and I continued to look for those things in the illegal drug market.

Over the next several years, I became deeply entrenched in street life, an unforgiving but undeniable education in survival, power, and leadership. The lessons I had learned in Tennessee, both the mistakes and the hard-earned wisdom, had sharpened me. I was no longer a reckless kid navigating the drug game blindly. This time, I was more prepared.

When I arrived in Pittsfield, Massachusetts, in the spring of 1995, I had nothing but a bag of personal belongings and the knowledge I had gained from my past experiences. Still under the mentorship of Rakim, I began hustling in Pittsfield. But the streets are unpredictable, and before long, in the fall of 1995, I was arrested on minor drug charges, spending several months locked up. That short stretch inside marked a turning point, not just in my business but in my partnership with Rakim. When I came home in 1996, we didn't part ways as friends, but we did part ways in business. I branched out on my own. We were still a team, but now, I was running my own product, calling my own shots.

And that was only the beginning. As time went on, I rose in status, evolving from the young kid who was once the mentee and the one being supplied to the mentor and the supplier. My influence stretched far beyond my immediate team. Before long, I was controlling 80 to 90 percent of the drug trade in Pittsfield and Berkshire County, Massachusetts. I was also expanding and reconnecting with cities and states we had touched before. First Tennessee. Then upstate New York. Then new states such as Maryland and Vermont, and beyond.

By 2001, I was at the helm of a multistate operation. The lifestyle followed: exclusive parties with music industry elites, luxury homes, spontaneous trips anywhere the team desired, top-of-the-line cars, designer jewelry, and women. We weren't just living; we were living the kind of life most people could only dream of. And I had built it all between the ages of eighteen and twenty-five.

The irony of it all was that while I was running a multistate operation on the streets, I was also excelling in college, living a dual life that few could imagine. My time at Moriah Military Camp reignited my love for formal education, allowing me to earn my GED. In 2000, out of both a deep respect for my mother and a genuine passion for learning, I enrolled in college in New York, the city where I was already spending most of my time.

Academics had always come naturally to me, and this was no different. I maintained a 3.7 GPA, proving to myself and others that intelligence and ambition were not confined to one world or the other. I never believed that being in the streets meant I had to be ignorant or uneducated. But what truly set me apart, both then and now, was my ability not only to navigate both arenas but to dominate them. That dual experience, the ability to move seamlessly between the streets and corporate spaces, has always given me an undeniable edge.

But I never got to complete my studies, and as I would soon learn, every empire, no matter how powerful, has its reckoning.

The lifestyle brought me wealth beyond what many could imagine, but the cost was far greater than I ever anticipated. Instead of lasting rewards, the return on that experience came as an unbearable debt, a price no one should ever have to pay. In the summer of 2003, everything came crashing down. I was arrested, this time, not for minor charges but for the kind of serious offenses that would seal my fate in the Massachusetts prison system. Local, state, and federal authorities moved in, arresting me for kingpin-level drug charges and firearm charges tied to conflicts with rival groups. One by one, they began rounding up members of my team from multiple locations, tightening the noose around our entire operation.

When the dust settled, the verdict was devastating. Without diving into every detail, the final outcome was clear: I was sentenced to 45–55 years behind bars. My empire had crumbled, and the life I had built was gone in an instant.

This was no juvenile detention center; this was the real deal. The stakes were much higher, the dangers more pronounced, and the lessons even more brutal. It was in this environment that I began to understand the power of communication more deeply. The prison system was a world unto itself, with its own rules, its own language, and its own hierarchies. To survive, you had to navigate these complexities with skill and precision. And it was also then that I realized there was power in self-knowledge.

By the time I entered the prison system, I had already attended two universities, unlike most of the men incarcerated there. I did not complete either program for obvious reasons. The duality of my life, one rooted in higher learning and the other in highly structured criminal activity, was rare in the streets and even rarer in prison. It set me apart and contributed to my rapid and steady rise in influence and power within the system.

In prison, your words can be your most potent weapon or your most dangerous liability. I learned to communicate with clarity, with purpose, and with intent. I learned to use my words to build alliances, to resolve conflicts, and to inspire change. Most importantly, I learned to use my words to reshape my own identity, to redefine who I was and who I wanted to be.

Armed with that wisdom and deeply rooted connections in New York's upper ranks of the gang world, while in prison, I found myself in constant communication with those who held real power within this organized underworld. Eventually, the opportunity came: a leadership position, offered directly by the Godfathers. After careful thought, I accepted. Under my leadership, I built the largest organized gang within the Massachusetts prison system and, ultimately, the state itself, with members in every jail and prison in the state, as well as most cities and towns in the state of Massachusetts.

Looking back, I now see how my vision and strategies, though executed with precision, were misguided and misdirected. However, every lesson I learned during that time became the foundation for the leader I would later become, the transformative leader I am today.

The Power of Storytelling

One of the most powerful tools in my arsenal wasn't strength, intimidation, or even strategy; it was storytelling. In the confines of the prison yard, stories weren't just words; they were currency.

They connected, entertained, educated, protected, and, most importantly, inspired.

I sharpened my storytelling skills, weaving together my past street exploits, the wisdom I had absorbed from books, and my personal experiences to shape the mindset of those around me. My drug empire on the streets was over, but inside, I was building something else, an empire of influence. Through stories, I instilled discipline, reinforced loyalty, and kept the men around me focused on a vision bigger than themselves.

One evening in the yard, a couple of young guys were getting reckless, moving without thinking, stirring unnecessary tension with another crew. They had the ambition but not the discipline, and in prison, the difference between the two could be the difference between surviving and becoming a cautionary tale. I needed to get their heads right, so I called them over.

"You ever hear about the time I lost one hundred grand in a single night?" I asked, leaning against the fence, letting them settle in.

That got their attention.

"It was back when I was still running things on the outside. We had a big shipment coming in, serious money on the line. But I let my ego get ahead of my discipline. I trusted the wrong man to move the product because he talked a good game, acted like he knew the streets as well as I did. But I ignored the signs, his desperation, his eagerness to prove something, and the way he ran his mouth too much. Sure enough, he got jammed up before he even made the first stop. Cops scooped him, and just like that, a hundred grand was gone. No product. No money. Just a costly reminder that, in this game, patience and wisdom will make you rich, but impulse will leave you broke or worse."

I let that sink in.

"You think power is about proving yourself every second? About making sure everyone knows you're the toughest in the room? That's how you lose. That's how you get caught slipping. The ones who last, on the streets, in here, and anywhere, are the ones who know when to move, when to sit back, and when to keep their mouths shut. They learn from every loss instead of letting it make them reckless."

They nodded, but I could see in their eyes that the lesson hit deeper than just words. I wasn't just telling them a story; I was handing them survival.

Through storytelling, I built trust, loyalty, and respect. My words became more than just entertainment; they became lessons, guiding those around me to move with intelligence instead of impulse. It wasn't just about keeping them in line; it was about teaching them to think, to believe in something greater than the moment. And in that world, that was the difference between rising and falling.

Effective Communication: Beyond Words

I also learned that transparency and honesty were critical. In prison, like in the streets, trust was fragile, and even the smallest hint of deception could have dire consequences. I made it a point to be upfront and truthful, even when it was difficult. This transparency earned me the respect and loyalty of those around me, a lesson that has served me well in every leadership role I've ever held.

But communication isn't just about talking; it's about understanding that every person has a unique story, a distinct perspective, and a set of experiences that shape how they see the world. As leaders, it's our job to listen, understand, and communicate in a way that resonates with the people we're trying to reach. And it's often through nonverbal cues that we convey the most critical parts of that message.

I learned to read people quickly, gauge their moods and intentions, and tailor my communication accordingly. I understood that effective communication was key to building trust, resolving conflicts, and inspiring action. It's how I built and ran a million-dollar drug empire by the age of twenty-one from 1998–2003, how I built and ran one of the largest gangs once incarcerated, how I helped build up, reshape, and run a 50–60 man platoon in a Military boot camp, and how I built, run and now manage a business portfolio worth millions today!

What I'm trying to help you understand is this: no matter where you are in life as you're reading this book, you can do it, you can make it happen. I've been in every situation you can think of, been involved in every type of lifestyle you can think of, and dominated. And I'm here to tell you that the same mindset, the same skillset, the same leadership philosophy that allowed me to dominate in one of those areas is the same that allowed me to dominate in all these arenas. And it will do the same for you.

Translating These Lessons to Leadership

As I transitioned into the business world, I realized that the core principles of leadership and communication are universal. Whether you're leading a corporate team, mobilizing a community, or commanding respect in the streets or prison, the foundation of leadership remains the same.

The most profound lesson I've learned, one that many fail to grasp, is that people are people, regardless of the environment. Whether someone wears a suit in an office, a uniform in a gang, hustles in the streets, or stands on the front lines of activism, we are all driven by the same fundamental needs. We want to be seen, heard, respected, valued, and understood.

Great leaders don't just recognize this truth; they know how to tap into it. They understand that leadership isn't about power, it's about influence. It's about speaking to the deeper needs of those you lead, earning their trust, and inspiring them to reach beyond what they believe is possible. This lesson was never more evident to me than when I co-founded and built the No Longer 3/5th Coalition.

In the midst of a complex political landscape, where organizations often found themselves at odds, be it for funding, political reasons, or sheer ego, I knew that uniting them under one cause would be no small feat. The fight against felony disenfranchisement in Massachusetts, especially regarding voting rights for the currently and formerly incarcerated, was a cause that required more than passion; it needed collective strength. My co-founders, Derrick

Washington, Leslie Credle, CEO and Founder of Justice4Housing, and I saw the necessity of forging a coalition that would be one of the largest in the state, a unified front comprising dozens of executive directors and their organizations, as well as individual activists and volunteers. But this wasn't going to be accomplished with just speeches or good intentions.

I understood early on that leadership in this particular space of community organizing wasn't just about talking louder or asserting authority. It was about mastering the art of communication, both verbal and nonverbal. Every interaction with an organization leader or activist became a dance of intention. I knew that in those critical moments of dialogue, what wasn't said was just as powerful as the words spoken. The subtle nods, the shared eye contact, and even the moments of silence were all part of the unspoken language that communicated trust and respect. These nonverbal cues broke down barriers when words alone couldn't. Active listening became my most powerful tool.

Often, the leaders of these organizations needed to feel truly heard before they could be willing to cooperate. The art of listening is not just about absorbing information; it's about making the other person feel seen. I listened not just for what was said but for the underlying concerns, fears of losing autonomy, frustrations with past collaborations, or even the reluctance to trust a new coalition. Empathy was key. By acknowledging these concerns, by reflecting back their feelings and validating their experiences, I could break through the walls of mistrust.

In one particularly tense meeting, an executive director of a major nonprofit expressed deep reservations about working alongside a rival organization. I felt the tension in the room rise, and rather than respond with immediate solutions, I sat in the discomfort, letting the emotions breathe. That pause, that moment of quiet, allowed for a shift. When I finally spoke, I acknowledged their long-standing differences but reframed the conversation around shared goals that transcended individual agendas. It wasn't about agreeing on every detail; it was about recognizing that the greater good required everyone at the table.

Through every meeting and every challenging conversation, I was constantly aware of how my body language either built bridges or reinforced divides. Sitting with an open posture, leaning in when someone was sharing their concerns, or standing back to give space, all of these cues played a crucial role in establishing an atmosphere of mutual respect.

Under the leadership of Derick, my colleague Leslie, and me, this coalition, "The No Longer 3/5th Organization," grew into something remarkable. We didn't just build an organization; we built trust. We turned competition into collaboration, and we did it by mastering not just the spoken word but the deeper, unspoken language of connection. This coalition is now a powerful force in Massachusetts, fighting for the voting rights of those who have long been silenced. It stands as a testament to the power of communication, both verbal and nonverbal, and to the leadership required to unite even the most divided.

Conclusion: The Lasting Power of Communication

As you've journeyed through these pages, you've witnessed the rhythms of communication in its purest, most raw form, facing sheer adversity, navigating the most complex environments, and building something from nothing. The lessons shared here are not just about mastering words or refining delivery; they're about understanding the deeper, untold truths that shape human interactions. In every exchange lies a moment of alignment, an opportunity to either strengthen or break bonds. And in leadership, that bond is everything.

True leadership isn't about titles or accumulated power; it's about connection, about making people feel seen, heard, and valued. It's about understanding the bridges that language can build, and the walls it can tear down. Ask yourself as you reflect on these lessons: How can you use your words and your silence to change the world around you? How can you build trust, inspire action, and lead with integrity in every area of your life?

The truth is that communication is the bedrock of everything. Whether you're leading a team, standing alone, or stitching together fragmented lives with shared purpose, your ability to genuinely connect is your greatest asset. This isn't a transaction; it's a commitment to empowering those you lead, and uplifting them with intention, wisdom, and empathy.

I stand before you now and tell you that no matter where you started, no matter the adversity you face, you, too, carry this power within. The words you speak, the silence you hold, and the trust you cultivate will leave legacies that last far beyond the moment. Leadership, in its highest form, is rooted in the authenticity of your communication. And with that, there is no limit to what you can achieve. So, take these lessons with you, and let your words, actions, and presence shape a future of influence, greatness, and enduring connection. Master the art, and the world is waiting for you.

Actionable Steps to Build a Culture of Communication

Here are some actionable steps that have guided my communication as a leader:

1. **Master the Art of Storytelling:** Use narratives to connect with your teams, convey your values, and inspire action. Stories are powerful tools that can make your message relatable and memorable.

   Example: Just imagine you're leading a team at a financial institution that's struggling to meet deadlines. Instead of barking orders like a boss, leaders inspire change. Share a story about a time you faced a similar challenge and how you overcame it. By framing your message through a story, you create a relatable experience that resonates with your team, encouraging them to push through challenges with resilience.

2. **Listen Actively and with Empathy:** Pay attention, not just to the words people say but also to their tone, body language, and what they don't say. Seek to understand their

perspectives and motivations. This builds trust and fosters deeper connections.

Example: Say you are in a fast-paced corporate setting, and a department head holds one-on-one meetings with each team member to discuss their concerns. During these conversations, they focus not just on what is said but also on the tone and body language. By understanding each employee's underlying motivations, the leader can address concerns proactively, leading to increased engagement and loyalty. Great leaders understand you can't have a one-size-fits-all approach and that each employee is a different person requiring a different kind of leadership at different times.

3. **Adapt Your Communication Style:** Tailor your message to your audience, considering their backgrounds, experiences, and communication preferences. Effective communication isn't one-size-fits-all; it's about meeting people where they are.

   Example: Imagine that you are a CEO preparing for an all-hands meeting that includes employees from multiple departments, ranging from entry-level to senior management. Instead of using corporate jargon, you tailor the message, making sure it's accessible to all levels of the organization. This ensures that everyone walks away with a clear understanding of the company's goals, regardless of their role. This may seem obvious, but I can't tell you how rarely it actually happens in organizations across all industries.

4. **Be Transparent and Honest:** Build trust by communicating openly and truthfully, even when it's challenging. People respect leaders who are honest and straightforward, even when the truth is difficult to hear.

   Example: You find yourself as a manager tasked with informing your team about potential layoffs. Instead of sugarcoating or withholding information, you choose to be open about the challenges the company is facing. By being upfront and empathetic, you maintain trust and respect from the team, even in a difficult situation.

5. **Use Multiple Mediums:** Leverage various communication channels to reach your audience effectively. This includes face-to-face conversations, written communication, digital platforms, and even nonverbal cues. The more ways you can connect, the stronger your message will be.

   Example: Imagine you are leading a growing organization during a period of change. You don't rely on a single announcement or meeting to communicate direction. You reinforce the message in multiple ways: a team meeting where people can ask questions, a follow-up email that clarifies expectations, informal check-ins to read body language and morale, and a visible presence in shared spaces that signals accessibility. Each medium reinforces the same message—trust, clarity, and alignment. When leaders communicate consistently across channels, confusion disappears, and confidence rises.

Leadership Reflection

1. Reflect on a time when your communication either built trust or damaged it. What did that experience teach you about leadership?

List up to five ways you can become a more intentional and effective communicator.

1.

2.

3.

4.

5.

The way to develop the best that is in a person is by appreciation and encouragement.

—Charles Schwab

CHAPTER 4

CELEBRATE SUCCESS— FUEL LOYALTY AND COMMITMENT

The Importance of Recognition in Leadership

Leadership is not just about vision, strategy, or decision-making; it's about people. And people thrive on recognition. A leader's ability to acknowledge, celebrate, and reward success is not just a feel-good practice; it is the fuel that drives loyalty, commitment, and high performance.

Think about it: When was the last time you felt truly seen and appreciated for your hard work? Not just a passing "good job," but real, meaningful recognition that made you feel valued? That feeling is powerful. It inspires people to go the extra mile, to stay committed even when the road gets tough, and to trust in the leader who took the time to recognize their contributions.

Too many leaders underestimate the power of praise. They assume that a paycheck is enough, that people should simply do their jobs without expecting anything more. But leadership is not just about results; it's about relationships. A leader who recognizes success, whether through verbal praise, symbolic gestures, or meaningful rewards, builds a team that is not only productive but also fiercely loyal.

I've seen leaders rise and fall in both the streets and the business world, and more often than not, the difference comes down to how they treat their people. Those who fail to acknowledge the hard work and dedication of their teams eventually find themselves surrounded by disengagement, resentment, and disloyalty. But those who make recognition a core part of their leadership philosophy build teams that will go to war for them.

In this chapter, we explore the undeniable impact of recognition in leadership. We examine why it matters, how to do it effectively, and how celebrating success creates a culture of loyalty and commitment that makes a team unstoppable. When people feel valued, they do not just follow. They fight for the vision. That is the mark of a true leader.

The Lesson of Recognition: A Turning Point

In the streets, success wasn't just about survival; it was about loyalty, trust, and the unspoken bonds that held our crew together. These weren't just words to us; they were the currency of our world, as valuable as any product we moved. When I returned from my first ill-fated trip to Tennessee, I was at a crossroads, unsure of what was next for me. It was Rakim, at this time, who first taught me one of the most valuable lessons I've ever learned—the true power of recognizing and celebrating the achievements of others.

He had charisma that drew you in and genuinely cared for his crew. He understood that true loyalty couldn't be bought with money or favors; it had to be earned through mutual respect, shared purpose, and, most importantly, recognition. The remarkable thing about him was that even our enemies liked him. I must say he had quite the personality.

What Rakim understood, long before I had the vocabulary for it, was that recognition is not a reward. It is a form of leadership currency. When people feel seen and valued, they don't just work harder; they protect the vision, defend the leader, and commit themselves fully to the mission. That was the turning point for me. I began to understand that loyalty is not enforced through fear or authority, but cultivated through acknowledgment, respect, and the intentional celebration of others. That lesson would shape every leadership decision I made from that point forward.

Building a Culture of Recognition: The Streets as a Classroom

As I branched out and built my own operation, the very mentors in the street who once guided me would, in time, become my mentees in the drug game, and I would ultimately take them with me on a journey to heights I never would imagine. With each step forward, I grew in stature, influence, wisdom, and power. Yet, I never lost sight of the early lessons I had learned; I carried them with me, honing them through trial and error.

With greater responsibility came greater challenges, but one principle remained unchanged: the success of my team was my success. I understood that recognizing and celebrating their contributions wasn't just about boosting morale; it was about fostering a deep-rooted culture of loyalty and appreciation. Sometimes it was a simple acknowledgment of a good idea in front of the entire team that could be just as impactful as a grander gesture. Sometimes, I rewarded an individual with something personal and meaningful, an expensive custom watch, a car, or high-end clothing, depending on what they valued. Other times, I extended that generosity to the entire team, reinforcing an unbreakable bond.

For some, I would publicly acknowledge a good sale, a clever strategy, or even a simple act of kindness. These moments of recognition weren't just empty gestures; they were powerful affirmations of one's value to the crew. As stated in the last chapter, I used nonverbal cues, such as a nod or a smile, to signal my approval and appreciation. These small, often unspoken gestures made people feel valued in a way that words alone couldn't achieve. Each acknowledgment, no matter how small, built loyalty and commitment to the cause. I made my team feel part of something bigger than themselves. That sense of purpose drove them to give their best every day.

As leaders, we often underestimate our influence. We forget how much our approval means to those who choose to follow us, regardless of the space we lead in. Understanding this was my greatest advantage. My team became impenetrable, untouched by enemies, and unshaken by law enforcement for a long time. Meanwhile, I watched other leaders fall, their teams crumbling under internal conflict, betrayal, or easy infiltration by law enforcement. The difference? Leadership that truly understands the weight of loyalty, recognition, and unwavering commitment.

There was a time when a member of my team, my homeboy Dice, who helped oversee my Maryland operation, found himself in a dire situation in Maryland and New York in 2001, caught by law enforcement and facing a case that could take everything from him. The authorities weren't interested in him; they didn't care about his future or what happened to him. He was just a pawn in their game. Their real targets were my second-in-command and me.

He had a choice: he could have given me up, cut a deal, and saved himself from years behind bars. It would have been the easy way out, the kind of decision most people would make when staring down the weight of a long sentence. But he didn't. He stood firm, refused to break, and chose to fight his case, no matter the cost.

Years later, I asked him why. Why, when given a chance to walk free, did he remain loyal? His answer was something I'll never forget.

"All my life, I've been forgotten. Overlooked. Taken for granted. Not even my own parents ever made me feel like I mattered," he told me. "But you, you were the first person to ever see me. To make me feel valued, respected, and worthy. For the first time in my life, I felt like I meant something. There was no way I could betray you. I'd rather go to hell before I did that."

That conversation was one of the most powerful and eye-opening moments of my life. It reinforced everything I believed about leadership, not just about treating people with respect, but about the limitless power of recognition. When people feel valued, they don't just follow you; they stand by you, even when everything is on the line. That's the kind of loyalty that can't be bought, only earned. And it all starts with how you make people feel.

Transitioning to the Corporate World: The Same Rules Apply

When I transitioned from the streets to the legitimate business world after my release from prison, I quickly realized that the same dynamics that fueled loyalty and commitment in the underworld of the streets were equally applicable in the offices of any kind of organization. People, whether in the streets or in corporate America, crave recognition, appreciation, and the feeling that their contributions matter. This isn't just a nice-to-have; it's a fundamental aspect of human nature.

Last year, I was hired to keynote for a conference in New York consisting of twelve large nonprofits, but it wasn't a simple speech. The hiring committee wanted tangible strategies for their problem. After my initial meeting with leadership, I, along with members of my small team, set out to conduct an anonymous survey with these organizations to get a pulse on the real issues. We even spoke directly to certain employees. The results were clear, and we knew immediately what could be done to address their issues when it came time for me to present at the conference.

As I stood before the assembled leaders and staff of these nonprofits, I could sense both eagerness and hesitation in the room. My message to them was clear: meaningful change in any organization starts with recognition, the true acknowledgment of the individuals who power every aspect of the work. My keynote focused on the impact of recognition, whether formal or cultural, as a driving force for employee morale, retention, and productivity. "If you're here to truly help your organization thrive," I began, "then you're here to listen, empower, and recognize the people who bring your mission to life every day."

To make my point clear, I proposed two pathways for them. First, implement a formal recognition program, a structured approach where achievements are consistently acknowledged and celebrated. However, I emphasized that if a formal program wasn't immediately feasible, they could start the second proposed pathway by creating a "culture" of recognition. Leaders and managers could actively choose to notice, praise, and appreciate their teams. The shift, I assured them, would be visible in their teams' attitudes and drive.

I conducted surveys after the implementation of these strategies. Before the keynote, the surveys revealed alarming trends—low morale, suffering retention rates, and lagging productivity among many of these organizations. The problem: a majority of employees felt undervalued and unnoticed.

After introducing either a formal recognition program or an intentional culture of recognition, the results were transformative. In a matter of several months, each organization, while having varying results as expected—saw morale scores improve by 10-15%; within the twelve-month range, retention stabilized and productivity increased by as much as 20% in some cases.

The second round of survey responses was filled with stories of employees who felt, for the first time, genuinely seen and valued in their roles.

One manager shared that a simple, consistent "thank you" had become a powerful tool in boosting team spirit and commitment. Another leader noticed that employees were taking fewer days off and engaging more openly in projects. The interesting thing that stood out to me was that the one or two organizations that implemented the second pathway, a culture of recognition, were met with similar levels of success as the organizations that implemented a formal program. This is a testament to the power and profound effect that recognizing and celebrating success have on the human spirit.

This experience underscored a powerful truth for every leader in that room: recognition is more than a reward; it's a reminder of purpose and belonging. When leaders recognize their people, they give them permission to thrive. It was a win-win because leaders witnessed the undeniable benefits of appreciation, and employees became more invested in the mission, knowing they were vital to its success.

I originally intended to use this situation, and some others, as a case study in this book, providing a deeper dive into the specifics, along with before-and-after data. I believed this insight would be incredibly valuable for readers and fellow leaders. However, due to many contract obligations that could not be waived for this publication, I am unable to share many of those details, and I fully respect that decision.

I make it a priority to celebrate the successes of any and all of my team members, both individually and collectively. The impact is immediate and profound. Morale soars, productivity increases, and a sense of shared purpose permeates the organization.

Celebrating success isn't just about giving out trophies or bonuses; it's about creating a culture of appreciation where everyone feels valued and part of the organization. It's about understanding that genuine acknowledgment delivered with sincerity and nonverbal reinforcement can be just as powerful as any monetary reward.

Connection Between Recognition and Long-Term Success

Recognition isn't just a quick morale booster; it has a lasting impact on an organization's long-term success. When people feel valued and appreciated, they are more likely to stay with the company, contributing to lower turnover rates. According to a survey by OnePoll on behalf of Bonusly, almost half of U.S. workers (45%) left a job because they felt unappreciated. Another 65% of respondents revealed that they would work harder if they felt their contributions were recognized by management.

Employees who feel recognized are more engaged in their work and feel more motivated to go the extra mile, leading to improved performance across the board. Moreover, a culture of recognition fosters resilience. When employees feel supported and valued, they're more likely to weather tough times and remain committed to the organization's goals. They understand that their contributions are appreciated, and this creates a sense of loyalty that can sustain a team through challenges. High employee retention allows for the development of deeper expertise, smoother team dynamics, and long-term innovation.

Innovation also thrives in a culture where recognition is the norm. When employees know their efforts will be acknowledged, they are more willing to take risks, suggest new ideas, and push boundaries. Leaders who recognize not only successes but also acknowledge the courage it takes to try something new create an environment where innovation can flourish.

The Role of Nonverbal Cues in Recognition

It is important to understand that recognition is not just about the words you say. It is about how you say them. Nonverbal cues, such as tone, body language, and eye contact, can significantly impact how your message is received. A leader's body language when delivering praise can either enhance or detract from the sincerity of the recognition.

For example, imagine a manager giving praise while looking at their phone or glancing at their watch. I saw this one day when I was with a friend of mine, Dan McCormick, CEO of a branding company with over fifty employees. One of his employees, Seth, secured a branding deal for the company, and as all three of us stood outside Dan's office, Dan proceeded to give praise and recognition to Seth. Unfortunately, he did so while looking at his phone, with his body turned away from Seth. I mean, not one time did Dan make proper eye contact with him. This half-hearted attempt at recognizing Seth's accomplishment undermined its potential impact. While Dan and I walked off, I couldn't help but notice Seth's body language; he appeared to be bothered by the half-hearted interaction.

I felt compelled to ask Dan about his take on his praise of Seth. He saw it as fine. He felt he had done a decent job of acknowledging Seth's contribution. To him, body language and a lack of direct eye contact were small and meaningless, a nonissue, instead insisting that his words were what mattered. He didn't recall any body language of Seth's that indicated otherwise. I, on the other hand, saw it as a significant threat to the overall well-being of his company.

Needless to say, I love my dear friend, but not even six months later, that employee left. He went to a competitor and took a valuable client with him—a loss that need not have happened. Dan ultimately hired my team and another team to consult and guide him and his company toward creating an environment that retains their talent. Implementing a solid recognition program, among other things, and training leadership to implement and maintain it has decreased their employee turnover and created a morale boost that Dan has admitted he had not seen before. Dan has since left his role at this company.

The point? Even if the words are positive, the lack of authentic attention undermines the message. Contrast that with a leader who makes eye contact, smiles warmly, and speaks with a tone that conveys genuine appreciation. The difference is profound. The latter leader not only acknowledges the achievement but also communicates that they are fully present in the moment, which amplifies the impact of the recognition.

Conclusion: The Lasting Impact of Recognition

In leadership, celebrating success is far more than a routine gesture. It is the heartbeat of a thriving organization. When you truly recognize and honor the contributions of your team, you not only fuel their passion and loyalty but also build a resilient culture grounded in trust, respect, and shared purpose. The stories and lessons explored in this chapter remind us that every acknowledgment, whether expressed through a heartfelt word, a sincere nod, or a well-earned reward, has the power to transform lives and elevate performance.

By embracing recognition as a core leadership principle, you cultivate an environment where people feel seen, valued, and motivated to excel, even in the face of adversity. This isn't just about boosting morale; it's about setting the stage for long-term success, where every team member's effort contributes to a legacy of excellence. Let this be your call to action: *commit to making recognition a cornerstone of your leadership,* and watch as it unlocks a future defined by loyalty, innovation, and unstoppable collective achievement. As we saw in Dan's company, small missteps in recognition can have outsized consequences, but when done right, the results are transformative.

Actionable Steps to Build an Environment of Celebrating Success

To truly fuel loyalty and commitment in your team, here are some actionable steps based on what I've learned:

1. **Recognize and Appreciate (with nonverbal cues):** Make it a habit to acknowledge the contributions of your team members, both big and small. Recognition doesn't have to be formal or elaborate; sometimes a simple "thank you" can have a profound impact. Remember that recognition goes beyond words.

   Example: Make sure your body language, tone, and facial expressions align with your message. Acknowledge achievements by being fully present, offering eye contact, and speaking with sincerity.

2. **Celebrate Successes Publicly:** Publicly celebrate achievements—both individual and collective—to foster a sense of pride and belonging. Whether it's a big win or a small victory, take the time to acknowledge it. Creating opportunities for team-wide recognition is essential, whether in meetings or through company communications. Public recognition reinforces that success is valued and celebrated by the organization as a whole.

   Example: At a monthly team meeting, the department head singles out one team member for their outstanding contribution to a recent marketing campaign. Instead of a simple mention, the leader spends a few minutes providing a deeper explanation of how the employee's innovative approach led to a 20% increase in customer engagement. This public acknowledgment not only boosts the employee's morale but also demonstrates to the rest of the team that their successes will be recognized and celebrated, creating a culture where people are motivated to excel. This is similar to one of the things I implemented at Dan's branding company.

3. **Offer Specific and Timely Feedback:** Provide constructive feedback that helps individuals grow and develop while also highlighting their strengths and accomplishments. Be specific about what they did well and why it mattered. Don't wait for formal employee reviews to give feedback. Offer specific praise right after successes. Give constructive feedback when it's due. Make sure to detail exactly what the team member did well and how it impacted the overall goals.

   Example: A project manager overseeing a software development team notices that one team member went above and beyond by fixing a critical bug before a client demonstration. Instead of waiting for the quarterly review, the manager *immediately* pulls the employee aside after the demo and says, "I really appreciate how you identified and resolved that issue with the software just before the client demo. It showed incredible foresight and saved us from what could have been an embarrassing moment. Your attention to detail directly contributed to our successful pitch." This timely feedback reinforces the employee's behavior and shows that their efforts are seen and valued.

4. **Build a Culture of Appreciation:** Foster an environment where everyone feels valued and recognized for their contributions. This isn't just the leader's job; it should permeate the entire organization. The best way to do this is to integrate appreciation into your company's regular schedule. Whether it's a weekly email, shout-out meetings, or informal check-ins, make appreciation a consistent part of your leadership practice.

   Example: A regional manager at a retail chain starts each weekly staff meeting by asking team leaders to share "Shout-Outs" for their employees. These are brief acknowledgments of appreciation for team members who went the extra mile during the week. Additionally, the manager sends out a weekly email highlighting standout performances or simply an appreciation of character traits across various locations. This routine becomes part of the company culture, ensuring that appreciation and gratitude are not occasional gestures but a regular part of the workweek.

5. **Encourage Peer Recognition:** Foster a culture where team members recognize and appreciate each other's contributions. In the same OnePoll survey mentioned earlier, 65% felt they would remain in a position with an unappreciative boss if their co-workers appreciated their work. This not only builds camaraderie but also reinforces the value of teamwork. Foster a culture where recognition comes not just from the top but from peers. Create systems that enable team members to acknowledge and celebrate one another's contributions, reinforcing camaraderie.

Example: This can be a positive post left randomly on computers or in face-to-face interactions. Leadership could implement something like a "Peer Kudos" program, as I did for the Coalition I co-founded, where employees can submit short notes recognizing a colleague's work. These are read aloud during weekly team meetings, and a "Kudos of the Month" winner is selected through peer nominations with a small reward: a gift certificate for a local coffee shop, etc. This system encourages team members to acknowledge each other's contributions, fostering a sense of *mutual respect and collaboration*. Over time, this peer recognition builds a strong sense of camaraderie and shared purpose within the company.

Leadership Reflection

1. When was the last time you felt truly recognized or appreciated by a leader, and how did it impact your loyalty, motivation, or performance?

2. Who on your team or in your organization deserves more recognition and appreciation?

List up to four ways you can become more intentional about celebrating others.

1.

2.

3.

4.

Trust is built with consistency.

—Lincoln Chafee

CHAPTER 5

HONOR COMMITMENTS—BUILD TRUST AND CREDIBILITY

A Crossroads in Leadership

In the realm of leadership, a promise is not merely a statement; it is a binding contract that reflects your integrity and shapes your reputation. Honoring commitments is the cornerstone of building trust and credibility, which are essential in determining how effective and lasting your leadership will be.

When leaders consistently fulfill their promises, they demonstrate reliability and steadfastness. This consistency fosters an environment where team members feel secure, knowing they can depend on their leader's word. Such dependability encourages open communication, collaboration, and a shared commitment to organizational goals. Conversely, when leaders fail to honor their commitments, skepticism grows, trust erodes, and morale and engagement decline.

Credibility, the perception of a leader's competence and trustworthiness, is directly tied to honoring commitments. When leaders align their actions with their promises, they build integrity and establish authority. They set the standard for accountability and excellence across the organization, making it easier to influence and inspire others.

Learning from the Best: A New Kind of Leadership

When it comes to leadership, trust, and honoring your word, I have to bring you back to Moriah Military Camp, which is the best example I've ever seen of people who live this principle every day. My transition from the chaotic streets to the rigid structure of the Moriah Military Program was jarring. The discipline, the unwavering hierarchy, and the constant drills and physical challenges were a world away from the freewheeling chaos of my former life. But I adapted, drawing on the resilience and adaptability I had honed on the streets.

Military-style training and living were a crash course in leadership. The strict regimen demanded precision and an adherence to principles that I had only touched upon in the streets. The environment was unforgiving, but it was also fair in a way that the streets never were. Here, your word was your bond. Trust wasn't just a concept; it was currency that could make or break you.

The academy's emphasis on structure, a strict regimen, and accountability provided a framework for effective leadership that resonated with my experiences on the streets. In both worlds, trust was paramount because lives hung in the balance. Whether negotiating in the streets, leading a military-style squad, or at the helm of a nonprofit or Fortune 100 company, your word is everything. Your reputation determines your success or failure.

The Unspoken Lessons: Learning from Experience

This military-style environment wasn't just about the drills, the orders, and the uniforms. It was about the unspoken lessons that came from living, training, and growing with others on the same journey. It was during these times that I found myself sitting on the grass, engaging in conversations with men who had seen more than I could ever imagine. Decorated Navy SEALs, respected generals, and honored officers weren't just teaching us how to be soldiers; they were teaching us how to be men.

One warm Saturday afternoon, I sat with my drill instructors on the sidelines, watching my platoon unwind during a game of football, a rare moment of calm that gave us time to breathe, observe, and learn. As the game went on, my mentors began sharing stories, each one seasoned with hard-earned lessons and experiences. I always listened intently, but that day, the conversation took a turn that would profoundly shape my approach to leadership.

One of the officers leaned forward, his gaze locked on the field. "You know," he began, "there's something I learned early in my career. Your word. It's everything." It's not just a promise to others;

it's the foundation on which they'll build their trust in you." He glanced over at me, his eyes carrying a weight that told me this was more than advice; it was a lifeline.

"Think about it," another instructor added. "When your team hears you say something, they are counting on you to follow through. It is not just words. It is a commitment. And if you break that, even once, it ripples through your platoon. You will see it in their eyes: doubt. When there is doubt, loyalty fades."

Watching the platoon out there, I saw what they meant. I realized that leadership was not simply about commands but about building the loyalty and trust that make every command meaningful. That day, I promised myself that every commitment, no matter how small, would be honored. My word would be my bond. It would be a commitment to my future teams. It would be a foundation built on integrity, one of the most critical assets I could bring as a leader.

This lesson became a part of me, a constant reminder that trust isn't given; it's earned and upheld through unwavering dedication to one's word. As I carried this lesson forward into my career, it shaped every relationship I built and every team I led. And, as my mentors had assured me, I saw how honoring commitments inspired trust and loyalty in a way nothing else could.

These moments of accessibility were rare but invaluable. They allowed me to ask questions, to listen to stories, and to observe the unspoken qualities that made these men respected leaders. It was in these quiet moments that I began to understand the deeper meaning of leadership, the power of promises, and the importance of follow-through.

Applying Military Lessons to the Streets

These lessons proved invaluable when I returned to the streets. Although these lessons were meant for positive life transitions, my young mind applied military leadership principles to my criminal organization, creating structure and discipline. I set clear expectations for my crew, communicated my vision with clarity and conviction, and held everyone accountable for their actions. I ran it like a wise general, and, in a short time, it grew into a multistate enterprise where everyone shared equally, creating a more efficient operation built on trust, loyalty, and shared commitment. My reputation for reliability and structure grew, solidifying my position as a leader in the underworld. Even as I thrived in this dangerous world, the seeds of ethical leadership planted at the academy quietly took root, though it would take years before I realized how they prepared me for leading in the business world.

Honoring Commitments and Long-Term Success

A key lesson I carried into the business world was that honoring commitments not only establishes credibility but also lays the groundwork for long-term success. When trust is established, it unlocks the potential for sustained performance and innovation. When your team knows they can depend on you to follow through, trust becomes the foundation for creativity, collaboration, and resilience; without it, teams grow hesitant and disengaged.

In a corporate setting, a CEO who consistently delivers on promises builds a reputation for reliability that drives business growth, employee retention, and stronger partnerships. This principle applies to smaller organizations and nonprofits as well: honoring commitments to stakeholders, donors, and team members strengthens the organization's ability to navigate challenges and achieve long-term goals. I learned this well from someone I consider a mentor and outstanding leader: Delta Air Lines CEO Ed Bastian.

In the landscape of corporate giants, few leaders embody the essence of loyalty and commitment to their team as fully as Ed Bastian. His journey in leading Delta from the brink of collapse to becoming the number-one airline in the world is a testament to the power of honoring one's word and embracing servant leadership. Delta's history hasn't been easy; the airline weathered crises that would have unraveled most companies: the aftermath of September 11th, the COVID-19 pandemic, and even the looming threat of bankruptcy. Yet through each of these challenges, Ed Bastian remained steadfast, living by the simple but profound philosophy passed down from Delta's founder, C.E. Woolman: "If you take care of your people, your people will take care of you." Bastian understood that Delta's strength wasn't in its fleet but in the unwavering spirit of its employees. With this realization, he placed himself at the bottom of the pyramid, not above his team but beneath them, uplifting them.

To win back the trust of employees and customers alike, Bastian embraced four key principles that every leader can draw inspiration from:

- **Curiosity:** He urged everyone to stay curious, ask questions, and challenge the status quo. This approach naturally led his team to innovate and adapt.
- **Culture:** He committed to fostering a strong, purpose-driven company culture and mission that valued people above all else.
- **Decision-Making:** He demonstrated how to be an effective decision-maker under pressure.
- **Listening:** And, most importantly, he is actively involved and listens to employees and customers.

Ed Bastian made a promise to keep employees involved and informed, listening to them every step of the way. This wasn't just a one-sided effort; he asked his team to trust him, even when the future looked uncertain. And in return, he delivered on his promises, famously dedicating the first profits not to management bonuses but to his people, a commitment that has emphasized profit-sharing with employees as a core commitment.

Ed Bastian's story reminds us that true leadership means being an "uncommon leader," and isn't about power or prestige; it's about empowering others and keeping the promises that bind a company together. The simple act of honoring his word built an unshakeable loyalty and resilience within Delta's workforce. Under his leadership, Delta didn't just survive; it soared. His example of servant leadership shows us that when leaders honor their word and commitments, they foster a culture of trust, loyalty, and excellence, enabling an organization to rise above even the fiercest challenges.

The Ethical Dilemma: Leadership Beyond the Streets

The military academy also instilled in me a deeper sense of ethical leadership. Witnessing the value placed on integrity and the consequences of broken trust, I learned that leadership isn't just about guiding a team, but it's also about leading with purpose and committing to something greater than myself. I started questioning the path I was on and thinking about what kind of leader I wanted to be in the long term.

The military program had taught me the power of promises and the importance of follow-through. But it was years later, in the depths of prison, that these lessons, in connection with self-knowledge and education, ignited a spark of conscience. I yearned for a different kind of leadership, one built on integrity, purpose, and a commitment to making a positive impact.

In the early days of Motivational Dreamers, I faced a pivotal moment that tested my commitment to integrity and the values I sought to instill in my company. Transitioning from a life on the streets to leading a consulting and professional speaking company was fraught with internal conflict. The allure of my past life, with its familiar codes and immediate gratifications, sometimes clashed with my vision of a purpose-driven future. Meaning, when a person comes from a certain way of life and thinking, from a certain environment, a certain code, and a certain survival mentality, change doesn't happen in a flash of inspiration. That's movie magic. In real life, it's messy. The pull of old habits and familiar thinking patterns, the ones that once kept me alive, didn't just vanish because I had a vision.

I don't want you to think this was some overnight journey to change familiar thinking patterns. However, I was resolute in my decision to leave that world behind and dedicate myself to helping others find fulfillment and purpose.

One particular incident stands out as a testament to the power of keeping one's word. We had secured a significant contract with a prominent client, a deal that promised to elevate the company's profile and provide much-needed financial stability. As the project progressed, unforeseen financial challenges arose on my end, leading to delays and mounting pressure from the client to the point that they threatened to terminate the contract and tarnish our budding reputation. We promised this client a deliverable that we didn't yet have the financial bandwidth to support because I underestimated the projected cost.

Internally, I grappled with the temptation to revert to old habits, shortcuts, and compromises that could quickly resolve the situation, but at the cost of our integrity. To be clear, I wasn't going back to the streets; that life was over, but I was entertaining the idea of getting the required money to solve the problem from those who were still in that life. The ethical dilemma was palpable: Should I prioritize the company's survival by any means necessary or uphold the principles that Motivational Dreamers was founded upon? I chose the latter.

I convened a meeting with my team, which at the time was made up of dedicated volunteers, and transparently shared the situation. I assured them that we would honor our commitments without compromising our values. Together, we devised a plan to address the client's concerns and financial challenges we faced to get the job done, working tirelessly to meet the revised deadlines without sacrificing quality or ethics.

Our unwavering dedication did not go unnoticed. The client recognized our commitment to integrity and keeping our word, and instead of severing ties, they extended the contract, expressing their trust in our capabilities. This experience not only solidified our relationship with the client but also fostered a profound sense of loyalty and trust within our team.

By keeping my word even in the face of adversity, I showed that leadership goes beyond rhetoric; it demands difficult choices that align with one's values and inspire others to do the same. This incident became a cornerstone of Motivational Dreamers' culture, cementing the belief that ethical leadership is foundational to lasting success.

Honoring one's word and commitments extends beyond clients; it is equally critical for staff and team members. In the formative year of Motivational Dreamers, the company operated solely on the dedication of volunteers who believed deeply in our mission. These individuals committed their time and energy without financial compensation, driven by my vision of inspiring others to find purpose and fulfillment.

During this period, I made a promise to the team: once we reached a certain level of success, their unwavering commitment would be rewarded with fair compensation. This pledge became a cornerstone of our collective motivation, especially as we navigated the inevitable challenges and uncertainties that come with building a new company.

Though doubts surfaced as obstacles arose, their faith in the vision and in my commitment kept the team united and focused.

When we finally secured our first couple of significant contracts, resulting in a substantial financial breakthrough, I honored my word. Before allocating any funds to myself, I ensured every team member received fair compensation for their dedication. This not only validated their trust but also reinforced the principle that honoring promises is central to building a resilient and committed team.

Prioritizing the well-being and recognition of those who stood by me underscored the power of integrity, fostering a culture that propelled Motivational Dreamers forward in its mission to inspire others.

The Lasting Power of Trust and Credibility

If I've learned anything throughout my career, it's that lasting success is built on honoring your commitments and leading with unwavering integrity. I didn't get to where I am by taking shortcuts or relying solely on flashy social media reels and endless self-promotion. Instead, I focused on delivering on my promises to my team, my clients, and the audiences I served nationwide. This steadfast commitment is what I call my *"reputation equity,"* a unique kind of wealth cultivated over years of showing up and consistently delivering results.

I want to be clear that there is absolutely nothing wrong with using social media, ads, chasing leads, or creating eye-catching reels; many have found success through these modern tactics. I'm simply sharing my path and what got me here, and, in fact, I recently made a commitment to engage more on these platforms. My journey is one of integrity and hard work, and I hope that by sharing it, you can find the path that resonates with you.

Motivational Dreamers, as well as the TEARS organization, alongside my real estate company and the 3/5th Coalition, is the result of that reputation. I've been blessed to help many kids go on to college and other fields they otherwise would not have had the opportunity to pursue. I've partnered with some of the most wonderful organizations for great causes. I've been on stages most people only dream about, speaking to everyone from Fortune 100 corporations, universities, nonprofits, and schools of all sizes.

I'm invited because people know that when I step on stage, or into their rooms, I'll deliver exactly what I said I would. I'll bring value. I'll keep my promises and commitments. The same reasoning applies to the many partnerships with organizations.

In October of last year, in Chicago, I presented to some of the world's top Fortune 100 companies on "Leadership Responsibility." It was a moment that, honestly, made me step back and think about where I started and how far I've come. After the presentation, I was awarded the Trailblazer Award for Leadership, a huge honor and a reminder that success built on integrity, trust, and commitment is the kind of success that endures.

For me, this journey has been about more than just professional achievement. Building a legacy and company based on value-driven leadership, one that gives back to communities instead of taking from them, is something I take seriously. I've been able to turn that "reputation equity" into real change, not only for my clients and their organizations but for people in communities across the country.

The truth is, it doesn't matter where you come from or what your beginnings look like. When you lead with honor, integrity, and a commitment to doing what you say you'll do, you build loyalty, trust, and excellence. The people around you, including volunteers, employees, and clients, will see you as someone they can rely on. That kind of trust brings real success, the kind that lasts.

I am living proof that if you're willing to honor your commitments, put in the work, stay true to your word, and keep your faith in your higher power. No matter how challenging the path, you'll get where you're meant to be. What God has for you, *no one* can take from you!

I started my journey as a high school dropout and even faced the harsh realities of a period of homelessness. I overcame the unforgiving and harsh realities of incarceration and street life. But that wasn't where my story ended. I earned my diploma, went on to study at some of the nation's top colleges and universities, and became a successful business owner, community leader, and a man of unwavering faith in a purpose greater than myself.

Today, I'm recognized as one of the most sought-after speakers and consultants on leadership, company culture, and overcoming adversity across the country. Achievements like these don't happen by luck; they're built through perseverance, vision, and an unshakable commitment to rise above every obstacle. My journey proves that with the right mindset, dedication, and faith in your higher power, no challenge is insurmountable, and no dream is out of reach.

Conclusion: Your Word, Your Legacy

In leadership, your promise is more than a mere utterance; it's a binding contract that defines who you are and shapes the legacy you leave behind. Throughout this chapter, we've journeyed from the disciplined grounds of Moriah Military Camp to the gritty reality of the streets, and finally into boardrooms where vision meets integrity. In every setting, one truth remains constant: honoring commitments builds trust and forges unbreakable bonds.

In those early days, amid the rigid drills and quiet moments on the grass, I learned that a leader's word is the currency of trust. When seasoned officers reminded me that "your word is everything," it wasn't just advice; it was a lifeline that would guide my every decision. Those lessons, born of sweat and sincerity, transformed my approach to leadership. They taught me that every promise, no matter how small, is a pledge to build something greater than oneself.

I carried that lesson from the streets, where structure once earned me respect, into the foundation of Motivational Dreamers. Back then, we were a team of unpaid volunteers, driven by purpose, not paychecks. I made a vow to honor their commitment, even when resources were scarce and shortcuts tempting. So, when our first breakthrough came, I paid everyone before myself. That moment didn't just fulfill a promise; it set the tone for a culture of trust that still defines us today.

I want this chapter to serve as a testament to the power of keeping your word. It's about the unspoken understanding that your integrity is your most valuable asset. It's your "reputation equity." When you lead with honor and consistency, you build a resilient foundation that not only propels your organization forward but also inspires those around you to strive for excellence.

Remember, it doesn't matter where you begin, whether on the streets, in a military camp, or at the helm of a Fortune 100 company. When you live by your word, you create a legacy of credibility, foster a spirit of loyalty, and, ultimately, transform challenges into stepping stones toward greatness. Your commitment is not just a promise to others; it's a promise to yourself, and that promise can change the world.

Actionable Steps for Leaders to Honor Commitments

To help you incorporate the lessons from my experiences into your own leadership journey, here are some actionable steps:

1. **Define and Communicate Core Values:** Clearly articulate your organization's core values and the commitments that embody your leadership philosophy. Ensure these values, such as integrity, reliability, and accountability, are communicated at every level of the company. This establishes a shared understanding of what it means to honor one's word.

   Example: Reinforce these values regularly through meetings, internal communications, and by integrating them into performance reviews.

2. **Lead by Example:** Demonstrate unwavering commitment to your promises in every action you take, no matter how small. Your behavior sets the standard for your team, showing that trust is built through consistent follow-through.

   Example: When challenges arise, choose integrity over expediency. This personal accountability inspires your team to adopt the same disciplined approach.

3. **Set Clear Expectations and Boundaries:** Establish clear guidelines and expectations, and hold yourself and others accountable for meeting them. Consistency in this area builds credibility and respect.

   Example: Imagine you are a project leader at a construction firm. You set strict deadlines and clear deliverables for an upcoming project. If a key milestone is missed, you immediately address the issue, help problem-solve, and reinforce the importance of accountability. Your consistency in holding the team to high standards fosters trust and respect.

4. **Communicate Openly and Honestly:** Create an environment where team members feel safe to voice their concerns, share ideas, and hold each other accountable.

   Example: Regular team meetings and one-on-one sessions can help ensure everyone is aligned with the company's mission and values. Encourage candid discussions about challenges and solutions, emphasizing that every voice matters. This culture of openness strengthens trust and nurtures collaborative problem-solving.

5. **Honor Your Promises:** Make decisions that align with your values, even when faced with tempting shortcuts. Follow through on your commitments, no matter how small. A leader's credibility is built on the promises they keep. Integrity is the foundation of trust and long-term success.

   Example: An Executive Director friend of mine at a large nonprofit organization promises her team that if they meet their fundraising goals, she will personally ensure they receive additional resources for their next campaign. When the goals are met, she follows through on her promise, reinforcing trust and loyalty within the team.

Ask yourself: Where have I overpromised and not yet reconciled it?

6. **Establish Clear Accountability Mechanisms:** Implement systems that track commitments and progress toward goals, ensuring transparency and mutual accountability.

   Example: Use regular check-ins, performance metrics, and feedback loops to monitor progress and address any lapses promptly. This not only reinforces trust within the team but also helps identify areas for improvement. Accountability transforms individual commitments into collective success.

Leadership Reflection

1. When people hear you make a promise or commitment, do they genuinely trust that you will follow through? Why or why not?

List up to four ways you can become more consistent in honoring your commitments.

1.

2.

3.

4.

It takes twenty years to build a reputation and five minutes to ruin it. If you think about that, you'll do things differently.

—Warren Buffett

CHAPTER 6

MORAL COURAGE — CHOOSING PRINCIPLE OVER PRESSURE

What do you do when the right decision costs you? The most dangerous moment in leadership is not when you lack skill. It is when you face a choice.

Most people think leadership is tested in the obvious places. In public moments, in performance, in pressure, and in competition. But the real test shows up in a much quieter way, and usually when no one is clapping. It shows up when you are alone with a decision that has consequences, and you realize that your talent cannot save you. Your résumé cannot save you. Your confidence cannot save you. You can be the smartest person in the room and still lose everything because skill is not the foundation of trust; character is. And when leadership is tested at the level of character, there is nowhere to hide.

That is the essence of moral courage. It is the discipline of choosing alignment over advantage. It is the ability to stand on principle when compromise looks strategic and beneficial. It is the willingness to lose something you want in the short term because you refuse to lose yourself in the long term. Moral courage is not the loud, cinematic version of bravery that people like to post about. It is usually quiet. It is usually inconvenient. It usually costs you something. And that is exactly why it matters.

Every leader eventually reaches a crossroads where competence becomes irrelevant, and conviction becomes everything. Whether you are in the streets, in a boardroom, building a company from the ground up, or carrying the responsibility of a major institution, the moment will come when the real question is not, "What can I do?" The question is, "Who am I willing to be?" In that moment, the difference between a leader who lasts and a leader who collapses is not intelligence; it is integrity. And integrity is not a mere belief. Integrity is a decision you make while something else is pulling on you.

The hard part is not always that you don't know what is right. Sometimes you know exactly what is right, and you choose something else anyway. Sometimes the real battle is not confusion; it is ego. It is pride. It is the fear of looking weak. It is the pressure of reputation. It is the temptation to protect your image instead of your integrity. Leadership is tested in uncertainty, yes. But it is also tested in clarity. Not only when you are unsure, but when you are certain and still must decide who you are going to be.

This was a lesson I had to learn when my leadership was tested in the streets.

When Pride Silences Principle

Years before Motivational Dreamers, before corporate contracts and conference stages, and before I had ever talked about moral courage, let alone understood it, I failed a moral test.

In 2002, a young man who worked under me in my street organization gambled with someone from another faction out of New York. He lost. Instead of owning the loss, he pulled out a gun and robbed the man to get most of the money back. In the streets, that is a violation. If you gamble and lose, you wear and accept it. That is the code. That is the order that keeps chaos from spilling everywhere.

At first, I did not even know it had happened. Months later, the tension surfaced publicly. The other guy approached us and began arguing in front of me. In that moment, instead of slowing down and asking questions, I did what my ego wanted me to do. I took my man's side automatically. Later that day, I got the full story.

And here is the truth: I knew it was wrong!

I knew the money should have been returned. I knew the right call was to correct it immediately. The older guys in my neighborhood who raised me would have forced that correction, not because they were saints but because they understood something I did not yet have the discipline to practice: small wrongs create big wars.

But I did not fix it.

I told myself we were not giving anything back. I told myself we were not going to look weak. I convinced myself that reputation mattered more than restitution. If I am being honest, it was not a strategy. It was pride. And pride is expensive.

That one decision created a snowball effect that led to indictments and had consequences far beyond the immediate individuals involved.

Because of my pride, my mother lost her youngest son to a prison sentence that was supposed to last fifty-five years. My daughter lost her father during precious years she will never get back. My fiancée lost the future we were building together. And it did not stop with me. Families on both sides of that dispute were fractured by a decision that should have been corrected in one afternoon. All because I did not have the moral courage to say, "We were wrong. Fix it."

That was not a strategy. That was not loyalty. That was not leadership.

That failure shaped me more than any victory ever could because I learned something the hard way. When a leader refuses to do what is right, the consequences are never private. They ripple. They multiply. They spread. When you are in charge, your failure to stand on principle becomes someone else's consequence. That is moral failure in leadership.

I did not lack intelligence. I did not lack influence. I lacked the moral courage to override my pride and do what I knew was right. And that failure cost more than I was prepared to pay.

What I did not understand at the time was that followers borrow their moral standard from the person at the top. When a leader rationalizes compromise, the team learns that compromise is acceptable. When a leader chooses pride over principle, the culture becomes pride-driven instead of principle-driven. Teams do not become corrupt overnight. They drift. And that drift usually begins with a leader's silent permission.

Looking back, it was a hard lesson, but one that shaped my approach to leadership. Now, I prioritize integrity over image, knowing the true cost of "compromise."

That lesson did not stay in the streets. It followed me years later into boardrooms, partnerships, and business contracts. Because leadership does not reset when your environment changes, it simply waits for the next decision.

When the Money Was Not Worth the Brand

In the building stages of Motivational Dreamers, when our vision was strong but our foundation was still fragile, we had purpose, we had momentum, and we had impact, but we did not yet have stability. We were still in that stage where every opportunity felt like it could determine whether the company would truly grow or quietly die. That is the stage where leaders are most vulnerable because pressure makes people negotiable.

Then an opportunity came that looked like the kind of break you do not turn down.

A well-known company approached me about a partnership. It was serious money. Not small money, not "nice to have" money. It was the kind of money that would have put us in a healthy position early, the kind of money that would have allowed us to scale faster, hire sooner, and operate with breathing room. On paper, everything checked out. The brand was legitimate. The offer was real. There were no obvious issues attached to it. There was no clear red flag that screamed, "Run!"

And I was ready to take it.

But my partner, Denise, said something that stopped me cold. She said, "David, this brand does not represent what we represent."

I did what many leaders would do at that moment. I tried to rationalize it. I told myself money is money and business is business, and that we could take the resources and still keep our mission intact. But the more I looked, the more I realized she was not talking about legality. She was talking about alignment. Their culture was built around dominance and profit at all costs. Their language was about crushing people to get to the top. Their focus was money, power, image, and leverage. There was no conversation about community. No conversation about values. No conversation about who or what gets built, who gets protected, or who gets made better. It was not just different from us. It was the opposite of us.

That is where the real temptation was because the offer was not obviously wrong. It was simply not us.

I lost sleep over that decision because that money would have changed everything. It would have solved real problems. It would have removed real pressure. It would have accelerated our growth at a time when we needed acceleration. And if I am being honest, I spent over a week wrestling with myself, trying to find a way to justify getting in bed with something that violated what I knew I stood for. That is what moral compromise does. It does not attack your intelligence. It negotiates with your ambition. It tells you, "Just this once." It tells you, "This is strategic." It tells you, "This is what a grown business is." It tells you, "You can clean it up later." And if you are not careful, you will sell your values in exchange for relief.

In the end, I turned it down.

Not because I had another deal lined up. Not because we were financially comfortable. Not because I wanted to look noble. I turned it down because I could not attach my name, my mission, and my company to something that did not reflect who I was, even if the price was high. That is moral courage. It is choosing to stay aligned when misalignment offers you a reward.

And then something happened that I will never forget. About six months later, that same company was under investigation. Financial misconduct. Fraud-related issues. Authorities got involved. The company collapsed. Some got into legal trouble. The whole thing imploded. And when I saw it, I thanked God, because I realized something that leaders do not always see in real time. Doing the right thing did more than protect my integrity. It protected my future. It protected my name. It protected my company. It protected my legacy from becoming collateral damage in someone else's scandal.

It also protected the people who would one day attach their livelihoods to our company. Every partner and every client trusts that leadership decisions are made with integrity. When leaders compromise at the top, teams pay at the bottom. Jobs disappear. Morale fractures. Loyalty erodes. But when leaders hold the line under pressure, teams gain something far more valuable than revenue. They gain stability and trust. And that is how you build teams that last in any environment.

Here's the truth that I had to learn from this.

Moral courage is not always tested when something is obviously wrong. It is also tested when a compromise looks strategic.

When the deal is legal but misaligned. When the money involved solves real problems. When the shortcut feels like wisdom. When the partnership is tempting and defensible. That is when leaders fold, not because they are evil but because they are tired, pressured, ambitious, or afraid. Most downfalls do not start with bad intent. They start with rationalization. A small compromise framed as survival. A value adjustment labeled as growth. A decision that is explained away, then repeated, and then normalized, until a leader looks up one day and realizes that they traded the very thing that made them trustworthy.

If you do not decide who you are before opportunity arrives, opportunity will decide for you. If you are not anchored in your convictions, you will bend toward convenience. You will choose relief over righteousness. You will confuse winning with being right. And when the consequences arrive, you will not be able to talk your way out of them, because the problem will not be your skill. The problem will be your choice.

When leadership is tested under fire, the ones who last are not the most gifted. They are the ones grounded in principle.

The Price of Compromised Leadership

That same tension between principle and profit does not disappear in corporate America. It becomes more dangerous.

In corporate environments, compromise rarely feels like ego. It feels like performance. It feels like growth. It feels like shareholder expectations, quarterly targets, and competitive survival. The language changes, but the temptation does not. The question remains the same: Do you correct what is wrong when it costs you, or do you protect momentum and hope the consequences never surface?

The mistake many people make is believing that moral collapse only happens in reckless environments. They assume corruption belongs to the streets or to immature leadership. But some of the most devastating failures in modern history happened in polished boardrooms, inside institutions filled with elite credentials and sophisticated strategies.

The names change. The environments look cleaner. The language sounds more refined. But the test is identical.

And when moral courage is absent at the highest levels, the consequences ripple across entire economies.

One of the most visible examples of this dynamic is Enron.

Enron did not collapse because it lacked intelligence. It was filled with some of the brightest financial minds in the country. It collapsed because leadership chose image over honesty. Losses were hidden. Risk was disguised. Numbers were manipulated to maintain the illusion of strength. Each compromise required another layer to protect it. And, at critical moments, no one exercised moral courage. No one stood up and said, "This is wrong. We stop now," even if it meant losing stock value or reputation.

When the truth surfaced, thousands lost their jobs. Retirement savings evaporated. Executives were led away in handcuffs. The collapse appeared sudden, but the real failure happened quietly, in rooms where leaders knew better and chose not to act.

Wells Fargo followed a similar pattern, though the mechanism was different. Unrealistic sales quotas created a culture where performance mattered more than principle. Employees opened accounts that customers did not request. What may have started as isolated shortcuts became normalized behavior. Leadership saw the numbers. The warning signs were there. But results were rewarded, and the system continued.

Moral courage would have meant confronting the culture early. It would have meant admitting that the pressure itself was corrupting integrity, even if profits dipped. Instead, compromise compounded. Billions in fines followed. Trust was fractured. Reputations were damaged.

These were not failures of strategy. They were failures of conviction.

And when conviction fails at the top, the people below absorb the damage. Employees who had no role in the compromise lose their jobs. Teams that worked in good faith lose their confidence in leadership. High performers leave environments where ethics are negotiable. The absence of moral courage does not just damage balance sheets; it destabilizes entire teams at every level.

I want to be clear: not every failure of moral courage ends in prison sentences, indictments, or billion-dollar fines. In fact, most do not. They look quieter. Smaller. Harder to detect. It looks like protecting a high performer who violates your culture because their numbers are strong. It looks like ignoring a pattern of disrespect because addressing it would create discomfort. It looks like adjusting standards to keep momentum. It looks like silence when something feels wrong, but speaking up feels inconvenient.

The scale may be different. The headlines may never come. But the impact is still real.

Corruption at scale rarely begins with evil intent. It begins when leaders recognize misalignment and decide it is not the right time to address it. It begins when short-term performance is treated as justification for long-term risk. Without moral courage to interrupt the pattern early, the damage multiplies.

When the numbers look strong but the foundation is cracked, collapse is only a matter of time. Not because markets are cruel. Not because competition is fierce. But because leadership without moral courage eventually destroys what it builds.

Whether you are in the streets, building a company, or leading a corporation worth billions, the test is the same. When you see what is wrong and you have the authority to address it, do you act, even if it costs you?

If the answer is no, success becomes temporary. If the answer is yes, you may lose something in the moment, but you preserve the only assets that sustain leadership over time: trust and integrity.

Conclusion

The streets taught me what happens when pride silences principle. I knew what was right, and I chose ego instead. The result was destruction. Lives disrupted. Futures altered. A leadership decision that should have been corrected in one afternoon became a chain reaction that could not be undone.

Building Motivational Dreamers taught me the same lesson under different pressure. This time, the temptation was not retaliation. It was an opportunity. The money was real. The partnership was legitimate. No one would have blamed me for taking it. But the misalignment was clear. And when I chose principle over profit, the result was preservation. The company grew on a clean foundation because its values were not negotiable.

Corporate scandals show the pattern at scale. When executives see the numbers, understand the risk, and choose profit over conscience anyway, the collapse is not accidental. It is cumulative. Wells Fargo did not open fraudulent accounts by mistake. Enron did not manipulate financial statements by accident. Decisions were made. Lines were crossed. Warnings were ignored. And eventually the damage spread far beyond boardrooms. Employees lost their jobs. Investors lost their life savings. Retirements disappeared. Executives went to prison. Reputations that took decades to build were erased overnight.

Different environments, the same test.

Leadership does not collapse because someone lacks talent. It collapses because someone knew better and chose differently. Sometimes the threat is ego. Sometimes the threat is money. Sometimes the threat is pressure. But beneath all of it, the question never changes: Who are you when it costs you?

Before the deal is signed. Before retaliation escalates. Before indictments are handed down. Before headlines are written. If you cannot answer that question clearly in private, you will not answer it correctly in public. That is the demand of moral courage.

Here is the framework I use now whenever I face a consequential decision:

1. Does this align with who I say I am?
2. Would I be comfortable explaining this choice to the people I love?

3. If this decision were exposed tomorrow, would I stand by it without flinching?

If the answer is no, the cost is too high.

Because what you build with compromise will one day collapse under it.

Actionable Steps for Leading with Moral Courage

1. **Define Your Non-negotiables in Advance:** Decide who you are before the pressure arrives. Moral courage is not built in the moment of temptation; it is revealed there. If you have not already clarified the values you refuse to compromise, you will negotiate with yourself when the stakes rise. Write down your standards. Be specific. Identify what you will not trade for money, influence, growth, protection, or pride. When your convictions are defined in advance, you avoid confusion when opportunity looks attractive but misaligned.

   Example: Imagine you are offered a high-paying partnership that would dramatically accelerate your company's growth. The numbers solve real problems. The brand is legitimate. Nothing about the deal is illegal. But something about the culture and language contradicts your mission. Before entering negotiations, you revisit your written values and compare the partnership to who you say you are. By deciding in advance what you will not compromise, you prevent yourself from rationalizing a decision that could weaken your foundation later.

2. **Correct Small Wrongs Immediately:** Small compromises rarely stay small. What feels minor in the moment can multiply into consequences that affect people far beyond the original decision. Moral courage requires addressing misalignment early, even when correction feels uncomfortable or costly. Delay often feels strategic, but it usually compounds damage.

   Example: If a member of your team violates a policy or acts in a way that contradicts your stated standards, address it immediately instead of minimizing it to preserve image or avoid tension. A leader who postpones correction often tells themselves that they are protecting stability. In reality, they are allowing a crack in the foundation to widen. Correcting a small wrong today prevents a larger crisis tomorrow.

3. **Slow Down When Pressure Is High:** Urgency has a way of compressing judgment. Financial, competitive, or reputational pressure can make compromise feel necessary. When the stakes feel high, resist the instinct to move quickly. Space creates clarity. Clarity protects integrity.

   Example: As an executive facing aggressive quarterly targets, you discover that adjusting reporting methods could improve how performance appears without technically violating policy. Instead of rushing to protect numbers, you pause and bring in legal or ethics advisors to evaluate the implications. That intentional slowdown may cost you a short-term performance boost, but it protects your credibility and prevents long-term fallout that could damage your team, your reputation, and your organization.

4. **Separate Ego from Principle:** Not every challenge to your authority is a threat. Sometimes pride speaks louder than wisdom. Moral courage requires the discipline to distinguish between defending what is right and defending your image. When ego drives leadership, correction feels like weakness. When principle drives leadership, correction strengthens trust.

   Example: During a conflict between two departments, you initially defend your team out of loyalty. Later, you discover that someone on your side was clearly wrong. Instead of doubling down to protect pride, you publicly acknowledge the mistake and take corrective action. That decision may bruise ego in the moment, but it reinforces a culture where integrity matters more than saving face.

5. **Evaluate the Ripple Effect, Not Just the Immediate Gain:** Leadership decisions are never isolated. The impact of your choice rarely stops with you. Before finalizing a consequential decision, consider who else may be affected and how far the consequences could travel. Moral courage means absorbing short-term discomfort to prevent long-term damage to others.

   Example: If your company has the opportunity to cut corners to boost margins or secure a competitive edge, evaluate more than the financial upside. Consider how that decision might affect employees, customers, stakeholders, and your long-term reputation. A short-term gain that compromises trust can eventually erode the very success it was meant to protect. Leaders who think in ripples, not moments, build foundations that last.

Leadership Reflection

1. What is one situation where you knew the right thing to do, but pressure, pride, fear, money, loyalty, or image tempted you to choose differently?

2. What did that moment reveal about your leadership?

3. Where in your life or leadership are you currently rationalizing something you know needs to be addressed?

4. What is one value you refuse to compromise, even if protecting it costs you opportunity, money, approval, or comfort?

The most basic of all human needs is the need to understand and be understood. The best way to understand people is to listen to them.

—*Ralph G. Nichols*

CHAPTER 7

ACTIVELY LISTEN — GAIN INSIGHTS AND BUILD RELATIONSHIPS

Listening Is Strategic Leadership

When I realized that every person is different, and that we are all motivated by unique forces, I began to tune in more deeply. Through intentional listening, I learned to uncover what truly drives people. Over the years, I've learned this principle in a variety of settings: the raw reality of the streets, the rigid structure of military-style boot camp life, the isolating corridors of prison, and the pressure-filled rooms of the corporate and nonprofit world. Understanding what moves people is one of the oldest and most powerful principles of leadership. I've said it a thousand times: "People are people," no matter their background.

From block corners to boot camp fields to boardrooms, the leaders who lasted longest weren't the loudest; they were the ones who listened the deepest.

That's why I believe that listening isn't just an act of empathy; it's a leadership weapon. It is a strategic tool that lets you gather critical intelligence and sense what's happening beneath the surface. Whether I was navigating a gang negotiation or a corporate decision, listening often made the difference between success and failure. It's the quiet force behind bold leadership and the hidden catalyst for transformation.

Growing up in the streets of Brooklyn, I quickly learned that survival required more than physical strength or street smarts. It demanded a heightened awareness and an ability to read people and situations with laser-sharp precision. You could be at a house party, scanning the room, and suddenly sense, "Okay, something's about to happen." That instinctive alertness, honed in an environment where a smile could be a mask for deceit and a handshake a prelude to violence, became an invaluable tool in my leadership arsenal.

In this chapter, I invite you to explore with me the transformative power of active listening. It's about more than simply processing words; it's about engaging with the energy behind them, recognizing the silent signals, and making genuine connections. This isn't just a tactic for negotiation or crisis management; it's the heartbeat of effective leadership. When you truly listen, you not only validate those around you but also unlock insights that can propel your vision forward. It is the bridge that connects diverse worlds, the key that opens doors to innovation, and the foundation upon which trust and relationships are built.

Let us dive into this journey together, where every conversation holds the potential to inspire and warn us. Every silence speaks volumes, and every listening moment lays the groundwork for a future defined by clarity, purpose, and unwavering leadership.

What Is Active Listening?

Earlier, we talked about how to *speak* so people understand you. This chapter is about the other side of that equation: how to *listen* so you truly understand them.

Active listening is not just a passive act of hearing words; it's an intentional, focused process, a profound engagement with another person's message on multiple levels. It is the conscious effort to understand, interpret, and respond to what someone is sharing, not only with the mind but with the heart. Active listening is about fully immersing yourself in the moment, putting aside distractions, and entering the dialogue with an open mind and a receptive soul.

It goes beyond the surface of verbal communication, reaching into the unspoken emotions, intentions, and truths that shape the words we hear. Active listening demands intentionality. It is the art of listening with our whole selves: our body, our ears, and our undivided attention. It means being aware, not only of the content of the message but also of the world beyond the words: the tone, the body language, and the energy the speaker brings.

In the chaotic world we live in, active listening is a rare skill that demands mental discipline and emotional openness, inviting responses that demonstrate a true understanding of what we've heard.

After receiving a message, the active listener offers reflective responses and clarifying questions, assuring the speaker that they've been understood while digging deeper into the conversation. In doing so, active listeners provide space for meaningful dialogue, where real relationships are nurtured, and real transformations occur. At its core, active listening is an exercise in respect and empathy. It's a commitment to understand and meet the speaker where they are, without judgment, without distraction, and without preparing a response while they are still talking.

It's about acknowledging that each person's words carry weight, emotions, and experiences that are worthy of our time and attention. To lead well, you must think and listen as others think and feel—even the unspoken. It is precisely in those moments of connection that the depth of true leadership appears.

Active listening isn't just for moments of crisis or formal settings; it shapes every daily interaction, from guiding employees and leading clients to navigating family dynamics and peer discussions. It's the bedrock on which respect, collaboration, and, ultimately, leadership are built. It unlocks insights into the hearts and minds of others, enabling a leader to see things from perspectives they might otherwise miss.

Active listening feels like a revelation because it opens the door to profound empathy and understanding. In a leadership context, it can lead to breakthroughs that transform teams, resolve conflicts, and foster unshakeable trust. It can also serve as a warning from those seeking to conceal their true intentions. It's not just about hearing words. It's about crafting a new way of being together:

engaged, rooted in reality, and catalyzed for action. In its purest form, active listening is the act of uniting, not just hearing but listening to connect, engaging fully with another's humanity. And that is how trust and loyalty are built—in silence and understanding as much as in action and speech.

The Cost of Ignoring the Unspoken

Reading people early on taught me that understanding others could mean life or death. In the streets, the culture had no favorites. You either adapt and survive or suffer the consequences. For my team and me, the rules were no different.

One day, my team and I were at a gathering in Maryland, a scene that masked a brewing conflict between a leader of another group and some of my Maryland team members. I decided to sit down with that leader to get a read on the situation and see if there was any chance to smooth over what was clearly a ticking time bomb.

Now, my homeboy Jay Black always carried himself with that "anybody can get it" arrogance. I've seen it too many times before; that kind of arrogance blinds you from seeing the full chessboard, the blind spots that tell you everything is not as it seems. I watched his body language, his eye contact, and the tone of his voice. Each told me the truth behind his reassuring words. Even though he kept saying that there was "no issue" and that "it's all love" between our teams, his energy said otherwise, and the way he shook my hand goodbye spoke a different language.

I walked back to my team and warned them that this guy wasn't a friend and posed a hidden threat beneath a calm veneer. I cautioned them, especially Jay Black, not to take him lightly. I come from a world where street kings got killed regularly, and I knew the cost of ignoring the signs. But Jay, caught in his own bravado, convinced himself everything was fine because the other man said that it was "all love."

As we parted ways, I urged everyone to head back to their side of town or go home, feeling it wasn't worth the risk in their territory. Some listened, but a few, including Jay, remained unconvinced. I left with handshakes and hugs, feeling the uneasy tug at my gut as we drove back to Massachusetts.

Just an hour and a half into the drive back, I got the call that shattered everything: Jay Black had been shot and killed by the very man I warned them about. An altercation erupted between our groups shortly after, and by then, it was too late.

The pain of that loss lingers to this day—the guilt, the questions. I replay every moment in my head, wondering if I should have pushed harder or even forced them to leave. But I wasn't that kind of leader; sometimes you have to let men make their own choices, even when the outcome is tragic.

It was a harsh lesson in the vital importance of active listening. In the streets, unlike corporate boardrooms, where the bottom line is money, your life depends on reading the room correctly. Ignore the unspoken signs, the body language, the hesitations, the truths behind the words, and you pay the ultimate price. That's when I understood: listening isn't soft. It's security. In street life, it can save lives; in leadership, it can save futures.

The Power of Active Listening

Satya Nadella's leadership journey exemplifies the transformative power of active listening, a story that reshaped not just a company but an entire organizational culture.

When Nadella became CEO of Microsoft in 2014, the company was at a crossroads. Years of internal competition and a "know-it-all" culture had stifled innovation. Instead of imposing top-down mandates, Nadella took a radically different approach: he listened, not only to boardroom reports but to every voice in the company, from seasoned engineers to entry-level interns.

Nadella began with listening tours across Microsoft's global offices. He attended team meetings, engaged in casual hallway conversations, and even joined virtual sessions to observe the subtleties of human interaction. With every conversation, he practiced what he later described as "listen more, talk less." This wasn't mere politeness; it was a deliberate, intentional effort to understand the hopes, frustrations, and ideas of his employees.

One memorable moment occurred during a regional meeting in Redmond. An engineer, normally reticent in front of senior management, hesitantly shared an idea that challenged the status quo. Rather than dismissing it, Nadella leaned in, asked probing questions, and encouraged a dialogue that refined the concept. The engineer's eyes lit up, not merely because his idea was taken seriously but because he realized that his voice mattered. This small act of genuine listening rippled throughout the organization.

Over time, a new culture of listening took root. Employees found that when they spoke up, their insights were not only heard but acted upon. This fostered trust and psychological safety. Teams collaborated more openly, innovation flourished, and Microsoft began reclaiming its place as a technology leader. Nadella's approach showed that active listening isn't just a soft skill; it's a strategic imperative that drives growth, sparks creativity, and enables breakthrough results.

Today, Satya Nadella's legacy at Microsoft is captured in his simple yet profound mantra: "Listen more, talk less." His story reminds us that when leaders truly hear the voices around them, they unlock a reservoir of talent and passion capable of propelling an organization to extraordinary heights. It's a powerful example of how the art of active listening can redefine leadership and cultivate a thriving, innovative culture.

What Satya did with engineers at Microsoft is what I had to learn to do with men and women in many facets of life: listen past the surface until people believe that their voice matters.

Listening in Leadership: The Common Thread

In my observations from the streets, the military academy, and the business world, the leaders who make the greatest impact are not those who rely on fear, intimidation, or rigid control. The most effective leaders earn respect through genuine care and concern for their people. They understand that loyalty is not a commodity to be bought with perks or titles but a bond that grows when nurtured with understanding, empathy, and attention to the individual.

Employees who feel truly heard and valued naturally become more engaged, motivated, and committed, not only to the success of the organization but also to the success of the people they serve and collaborate with. Leaders who actively listen, recognize contributions, and respond with empathy create an environment where trust, collaboration, and loyalty flourish. It's not just about management; it's about building a culture where people feel empowered to do their best work.

A leader who dismisses concerns or ignores the perspectives of their team risks alienating those very people they rely on to succeed. A title only buys you time to either increase your influence or undermine it. True leadership is about connection: understanding the unique motivations, ambitions, and challenges of each person and leveraging that understanding to inspire and elevate them.

Creating a Safe Space for Communication

My journey has taught me that the most effective leaders are those who truly listen. They create spaces where open communication is encouraged, where feedback is welcomed, and where diverse perspectives are not just tolerated but actively valued. They understand that building a loyal, high-functioning team starts with making each individual feel genuinely seen, heard, and appreciated.

In practical terms, this means fostering an environment where people can express their thoughts and concerns without fear of judgment or repercussion. It's about being approachable, accessible, and, most importantly, open to hearing the truth, even when that truth is uncomfortable. This approach builds trust and empowers teams to contribute their best ideas, knowing that their voices truly matter.

In the bustling world of leading organizations with diverse teams of employees and volunteers, I've learned that the essence of true leadership lies in active listening and empathy. This principle came alive for me in a pivotal moment while building Motivational Dreamers and the TEARS Organization.

Recognizing the value of feedback, I initiated a survey, inviting everyone from my small team, comprising employees and volunteers alike, to share their thoughts on the workplace, daily operations, and, more pointedly, leadership. I asked questions like: *What do we do well? Where do we fall short? How does leadership impact your ability to thrive here?* I didn't sugarcoat the intention behind the survey; I genuinely sought the truth, even if it stung.

When the results came in, I dedicated time to comb through every comment, both the praise and the critiques. Some feedback highlighted strengths, like how supported the team felt during challenging projects. Other insights were tougher to hear, pointing out areas where communication or decision-making could improve among those I had in leadership positions.

Instead of brushing off the difficult feedback, I saw it as an opportunity to grow. I called a meeting with my leadership team to discuss the survey's findings. We created a safe, open environment where no voice was too small to be heard. Together, we identified actionable changes, from improving communication channels to creating better recognition systems for volunteers.

But here's the key: as a leader, I didn't just ask for their opinions; I showed them I valued their input and acted on it. By owning the shortcomings and demonstrating a commitment to active listening, empathy, and transparency, I fostered trust and strengthened our team bond. In that moment, I wasn't just their leader; I was a servant to their success, embodying the essence of true leadership.

That survey wasn't just a tool; it was an act of respect. It told my team, 'Your experience here matters enough to change how we lead.'

Active listening isn't just about hearing words; it's about hearing hearts. Empathy transforms tough feedback into a tool for transformation, both for me as a leader and for the organizations and people I guide. This process doesn't just create better workplaces; it creates lasting relationships built on mutual respect, understanding, and shared purpose.

Conclusion: The Resonance of True Listening

As we close this chapter, remember: active listening isn't just a technique; it's the heartbeat of transformative leadership. It transcends environments, from the hard corners of the streets, where misreading a gesture could have serious consequences, to the sleek boardrooms of corporate America, where a misheard concern can derail entire initiatives. Across every context, active listening has remained my compass, guiding me toward empathy, clarity, and a lasting, meaningful impact.

Every conversation holds the potential to inspire, to build trust, and to uncover what lies beneath the surface. On the streets of Brooklyn, heightened awareness and attention to unspoken signals could mean the difference between safety and danger. In corporate environments, like Microsoft under Satya Nadella's listening tours, understanding unspoken concerns reshaped organizational culture and performance. One truth spans both worlds: true listening is the bedrock of effective leadership.

When we listen with our whole selves, we move beyond words. We listen with mind, heart, and intuition. We begin to read silent cues, understand the emotions beneath the message, and create environments where every person feels genuinely seen, heard, and valued. This is how leaders transform a group of individuals into a cohesive, empowered collective capable of innovation, collaboration, healing, and profound connection.

In leadership, every dialogue is an opportunity to connect, and every silence is a signal to decode. By embracing active listening, leaders do more than gather information; they shape organizational culture, deepen trust, and proactively prevent missteps that can escalate into crises. Let this principle be your guiding truth: extraordinary leadership is not measured by how loudly you speak, but by how deeply, attentively, and empathetically you listen.

Actionable Steps for Leaders to Build Active Listening Skills

To master the art of listening and use it as a tool to build stronger relationships, gain valuable insights, and cultivate trust, here are concrete, actionable steps you can start implementing immediately:

1. **Practice Active Listening:** Put away distractions, focus on the speaker, and show engagement through both verbal and nonverbal cues. Lean in, maintain eye contact, nod, and paraphrase to confirm understanding. Demonstrate that you are fully present in the conversation.

   Example: During a one-on-one performance review, a manager notices an employee hesitating to share concerns. The manager silences their phone, closes their laptop, and leans forward with open body language. As the employee speaks, the manager paraphrases: "So, you're saying the new project management software feels overwhelming because of the learning curve?" Feeling genuinely heard, the employee opens up fully, leading to a productive discussion and actionable training solutions.

2. **Ask Open-Ended and Insightful Questions:** Encourage deeper conversations and uncover insights by asking questions that go beyond "yes" or "no." Challenge your team to think critically and reflect deeply.

   Example: In a team brainstorming session, instead of asking, "Do you like this idea?" a leader asks, "How could this solution impact our long-term goals?" or

"What obstacles might we encounter if we take this approach?" These questions spark richer dialogue, prompting team members to explore multiple perspectives, anticipate challenges, and uncover opportunities that may have otherwise been overlooked.

3. **Create a Safe Space for Feedback:** Foster an environment where team members feel comfortable sharing thoughts and concerns without fear of judgment or reprisal. Lead by example: share your own experiences and vulnerabilities to normalize open communication.

   Example: After implementing a major organizational change, a CEO hosts an anonymous feedback session. In a follow-up meeting, they model vulnerability by saying, "When I first became CEO, I struggled with delegation because I felt the need to control outcomes. Please let me know if you feel I'm micromanaging." By demonstrating openness, the CEO builds trust and encourages candid feedback.

4. **Seek Feedback Regularly:** Solicit feedback, both formally and informally—and respond with visible actions. Show that you value input and are willing to grow.

   Example: A project manager distributes a post-project survey, asking questions such as:

   - "What aspects of this project worked well?"
   - "How could I have supported you more effectively?"

   If a team member mentions that frequent meetings disrupted workflow, the manager adjusts the schedule for the next project accordingly. This demonstrates responsiveness and reinforces a culture of continuous improvement.

5. **Show Empathy and Understanding:** Step into the shoes of your team members. Acknowledge emotions and validate experiences before offering solutions. Empathetic listening strengthens relationships and encourages open, honest communication.

   Example: When an employee shares that they're struggling with burnout due to personal challenges, a supervisor first listens fully, then responds: "That sounds incredibly overwhelming. I can see why it's difficult to focus at work. How can I best support you at this moment?" This validates the employee's experience and opens a door to discussing flexible arrangements or additional resources.

6. **Recognize Individual Differences:** Understand that what motivates one person may not motivate another. Tailor recognition, communication, and support to meet each team member's unique preferences.

   Example: A leader manages two employees with distinct motivators: one thrives on public recognition; the other prefers quiet acknowledgment. After a major project, the leader praises the first employee in a team meeting and sends a private thank-you note to the second. Both feel valued and motivated because their unique preferences were recognized.

7. **Encourage Peer-to-Peer Listening:** Build a culture where team members actively listen to and support one another.

Peer-to-peer listening reinforces active listening as a shared value within the organization.

Example: In a cross-functional team meeting, a leader introduces a practice: "Before responding, summarize what the previous speaker said to ensure you fully understand their perspective." After an engineer explains why a feature isn't feasible, the marketer responds: "If I understand you correctly, you're saying the timeline for this feature would push back the launch date. Is that right?" This method reduces misunderstandings, fosters mutual respect, and strengthens team cohesion.

Leadership Reflection

1. Do people around you genuinely feel heard when they speak to you, or do they feel like you are simply waiting for your turn to respond? What behaviors support your answer?

2. When was the last time you created a safe space for someone to speak honestly, especially when the truth was uncomfortable or critical of you as a leader?

List up to four ways you can become a better active listener.

1.

2.

3.

4.

The role of leaders in a coaching culture is to foster an environment of trust, collaboration, and continuous learning.

—John Mattone

CHAPTER 8

DEVELOP OTHERS TO LEAD— THE POWER OF COACHING IN LEADERSHIP

In an era where innovation and adaptability define success, leaders are under immense pressure to deliver results in ways that inspire excellence, foster engagement, and unlock potential. The pivotal question becomes: How can leaders create environments where people truly thrive, not just survive? Enter the coaching culture, a transformative approach that reshapes not only how we work but how we connect, learn, and grow together. Whether it's empowering a junior team member to lead a project or guiding a community initiative to success, coaching culture turns potential into performance.

In previous chapters, we focused on how leaders communicate, listen, and honor their word. A coaching culture is where all of that comes together. It is what happens when leaders use communication, listening, and integrity, not just to lead people but to develop them.

Unlike traditional leadership models that prioritize control and outcomes, a coaching culture emphasizes continuous growth, mutual support, and the development of individuals as whole people. It shifts the paradigm from a command-and-control approach to one of empowerment and collaboration. Here, every interaction, from a one-on-one check-in to a team brainstorming session—is an opportunity for learning. Every challenge is a chance to grow, and every success, like a project milestone celebrated across the team, is a shared triumph.

At its heart, a coaching culture recognizes that people are not cogs in a machine, but dynamic individuals with untapped potential. Leaders embracing this approach don't need to have all the answers; they ask thoughtful questions, like, "What's one way you'd approach this differently?" to cultivate trust and create an environment where others feel safe to explore, innovate, and contribute their best selves.

This mindset extends far beyond corporate boardrooms and office spaces. It thrives in nonprofits, community initiatives, schools, and even family dynamics. Anywhere that people interact and grow, coaching principles apply. In a world where connection and purpose matter more than ever, a coaching culture provides a blueprint for success that is as human as it is strategic, whether guiding a youth mentoring program or leading a corporate innovation team.

In the pages ahead, we'll explore why this shift in leadership is not just timely but essential. We'll define a coaching culture, explore its benefits, and, most importantly, show how to bring it to life, whether in a corporation, a grassroots movement, or the nonprofit sector. Adopting a coaching culture is more than a choice; it's a catalyst for meaningful, sustainable transformation.

What Is a Coaching Culture?

At its core, a coaching culture is a collective mindset in which principles such as active listening, constructive feedback, and developmental conversations are woven into daily interactions. Leaders and team members alike adopt a coach-like approach, whether it's guiding a colleague through a problem or asking questions that help them discover solutions themselves, fostering trust, accountability, and open communication.

A coaching culture transcends hierarchy. Instead of dictating or micromanaging, leaders inspire teams to think critically, solve problems independently, and grow both personally and professionally. As John Whitmore, author of *Coaching for Performance*, said, "Coaching is unlocking people's potential to maximize their own performance. It is helping them to learn rather than teaching them." This philosophy underscores coaching culture: an environment grounded in empathy, respect, and continuous growth.

A coaching culture is more than a leadership strategy; it is a paradigm shift in how organizations operate. It rejects the old top-down model and embraces collaboration and empowerment. Every interaction, from team huddles to client debriefs, is a growth opportunity for both the individual and the organization. Curiosity, learning, and collaboration become default behaviors, and people are encouraged to take ownership of their development and decisions, such as proposing a new workflow or mentoring a peer.

In a coaching culture, success isn't just about hitting targets or meeting deadlines; it's about developing people holistically. It's creating an ecosystem where individuals feel valued, teams collaborate effectively, and organizations thrive sustainably. When employees feel heard and respected, they're more likely to generate innovative solutions, like a team designing a new product or improving client services that reflect their unique insights.

Leadership in a coaching culture isn't reserved for formal titles. Anyone can adopt a coaching mindset. A frontline employee mentoring a teammate on a new software tool, or a community leader facilitating collaboration among diverse stakeholders, are all tangible examples of coaching culture in action.

A coaching culture is rooted in emotional intelligence. Leaders and team members cultivate self-awareness, empathy, and the ability to navigate complex dynamics. It's about meeting people where they are, listening carefully when a colleague struggles with a project, and helping them unlock potential. Leaders show vulnerability and humility, setting aside assumptions and learning alongside those whom they coach.

At its best, a coaching culture creates a ripple effect. When individuals feel supported and empowered, they naturally extend encouragement to others. A manager who coaches a team member may inspire that person to mentor a colleague, who, in turn, supports someone else. This ripple effect transforms organizations, communities, and families into interconnected networks of trust and growth.

In a world that is increasingly complex and fast-paced, the need for coaching cultures has never been greater. As psychologist Carol Dweck highlights in her groundbreaking work on the growth mindset, "Effort is what ignites that ability and turns it into accomplishment." A coaching culture nurtures this effort, encouraging people to embrace challenges, learn from feedback, and continuously strive for improvement.

Ultimately, a coaching culture is not just a set of practices or tools; it is a way of being. It is an intentional commitment to seeing and nurturing the potential in others, building relationships that are rooted in respect and authenticity, and creating spaces where people feel empowered to be their best selves. It is as much about heart as it is about strategy, and its impact is both transformational and enduring.

Why Is a Coaching Culture Important?

The importance of a coaching culture lies in its ability to address some of the most pressing challenges faced by leaders today: disengaged teams, high turnover, limited innovation, and fractured communication. In workplaces, this approach empowers individuals and teams by encouraging them to take ownership of their work and decisions. Instead of relying solely on directives, team members become proactive contributors to success. This sense of empowerment translates into higher job satisfaction, stronger engagement, and a greater willingness to innovate.

Trust is another critical aspect. Trust forms the foundation of any thriving organization or community. In a coaching culture, leaders demonstrate empathy and a genuine investment in others' success. This builds a high-trust environment that fosters deep engagement. When team members feel seen, heard, and respected, they are more willing to take initiative, offer solutions, and hold themselves accountable.

A coaching culture also promotes innovation by encouraging people to feel safe expressing ideas and taking calculated risks. When employees or team members know their voices are valued and mistakes are viewed as opportunities to learn, creativity flourishes. Furthermore, leaders who adopt a coaching mindset ensure sustainability by developing future leaders. By equipping the next generation with the skills and confidence to lead, coaching cultures contribute to long-term organizational and societal success.

The Benefits of a Coaching Culture

A coaching culture is not only transformative for individuals but also for the collective environment in which it exists. Enhanced performance and productivity are among its most tangible benefits. When individuals are guided to identify their strengths and address their challenges constructively, their contributions to the group become more impactful. This deliberate development fosters both individual achievement and collective excellence.

Employee retention also improves significantly in organizations that embrace coaching. People are far more likely to remain in environments where they feel valued, heard, and supported in their growth. This sense of belonging turns the workplace into a space of opportunity rather than stagnation.

Another advantage of a coaching culture is improved collaboration and teamwork. When dialogue is open, and team members are encouraged to support each other's development, a sense of unity and shared purpose emerges. Relationships between individuals strengthen, and collective problem-solving becomes the norm.

Beyond productivity and engagement, coaching cultures have a profound impact on mental health and well-being. Feeling supported and understood reduces stress, increases resilience, and leads to higher overall job satisfaction. This impact is not confined to professional settings; households that embrace coaching principles often experience similar improvements in family dynamics.

Ultimately, a coaching culture aligns personal growth with broader organizational or community goals. By integrating individual development into the broader vision, coaching creates a cohesive strategy for success that benefits all stakeholders involved.

Developmental Conversations: Key to a Coaching Culture

At the heart of every thriving coaching culture lies one essential practice: **developmental conversations**. These are not routine check-ins or performance reviews. They are *future-focused, growth-oriented dialogues* that empower individuals to reflect, dream, and act with purpose. Developmental conversations prioritize *who a person is becoming*, not just what they've done.

Unlike traditional feedback sessions, which often zero in on past mistakes or current metrics, developmental conversations are rooted in *possibility*. They're collaborative by nature, guided by curiosity rather than critique. These conversations invite employees to explore their goals, identify their strengths, navigate their challenges, and co-create a path forward, together with their leaders or peers.

What makes developmental conversations so powerful is their emotional and strategic depth. They signal to employees:

> *"You are not just a role. You are a person with potential, and we're invested in your journey."*

In practice, these conversations often include:

- Open-ended questions like "Where do you see yourself growing this year?" or "What's one skill you'd love to develop?"
- A safe, supportive space where honest reflection is encouraged.
- A leader who listens more than they speak, acting as a thought partner rather than a fixer.
- Action steps that align personal development with organizational goals.

When consistently practiced, developmental conversations become cultural cornerstones. They drive engagement, boost morale, and cultivate trust because people feel seen, heard, and valued beyond their output. In return, organizations benefit from higher retention, increased innovation, and stronger leadership pipelines.

In short, developmental conversations are not a luxury; they are a *strategic necessity* in any organization committed to long-term growth. When employees are invited into conversations about their future, they don't just perform, they *transform*. And so does the culture around them.

Coaching Culture in Different Settings

The principles of a coaching culture are remarkably versatile, applicable across diverse communities, nonprofits, corporate organizations, and households. In each of these settings, coaching creates environments where individuals feel valued, empowered, and capable of reaching their full potential. Let's explore how this culture takes shape in these different contexts.

Nonprofit Organizations: Fostering Passion and Resilience

Nonprofit organizations thrive on passion, purpose, and collaboration, but without proper support structures and coaching practices, these same qualities can lead to burnout and disengagement. A coaching culture provides a framework for channeling this passion into sustainable, impactful work.

For example, consider a nonprofit focused on youth development. By training mentors to adopt coaching techniques, such as asking powerful questions, listening without judgment, and encouraging self-reflection. The organization empowers young people to develop critical thinking skills and a sense of independence. Instead of merely providing solutions, mentors guide youth in discovering their own answers, fostering ownership of their growth.

This approach also has a profound impact on the staff and volunteers who drive nonprofit missions. When leaders in these organizations embrace coaching principles, they create a culture of mutual support and continuous learning. Employees feel heard and valued, leading to increased job satisfaction, resilience, and a deeper commitment to the cause. As author Simon Sinek aptly puts it, "Working hard for something we don't care about is called stress; working hard for something we love is called passion." Coaching culture helps transform stress into sustained passion by building strong, empathetic connections throughout the organization.

Corporate Settings: Unlocking Innovation and Retaining Talent

In the corporate world, where competition and innovation are paramount, a coaching culture can be a game-changer. Companies that prioritize growth and learning over rigid hierarchies often find themselves better positioned to adapt to change and attract top talent.

For example, Indra Nooyi, former CEO of PepsiCo, exemplified a coaching culture by actively mentoring her leadership team and embedding a growth mindset across the organization. She encouraged leaders to focus on development, not just results, asking powerful questions, giving constructive feedback, and fostering collaboration to unlock potential at every level.

Under her leadership, employees were empowered to take ownership of their ideas, experiment safely, and learn from mistakes. This created an environment where innovation thrived and engagement soared. Nooyi's philosophy demonstrates that coaching culture is not about titles or hierarchy; it's about leaders intentionally guiding, listening, and supporting others to grow while aligning individual development with organizational goals.

A coaching culture in corporate settings doesn't just benefit employees; it also enhances the customer experience. When leaders invest in their teams' development, they create an environment where employees feel motivated to go above and beyond, resulting in improved products, services, and client relationships. Ultimately, a coaching culture is about recognizing that the success of a company lies in its people. As Satya Nadella himself has said, "The C in CEO stands for culture."

Community Leadership: Inspiring Collective Action

In community leadership, adopting coaching principles can inspire collective action and build trust across diverse groups. Communities are often composed of individuals with differing perspectives, needs, and goals, which can create challenges when trying to drive change. A coaching culture equips leaders with tools to unite these diverse voices around shared objectives.

For instance, a community leader who adopts a coaching mindset prioritizes active listening and inclusive dialogue, ensuring that everyone feels heard and respected. This approach builds trust and fosters a sense of ownership among community members, making it easier to mobilize collective action. Instead of dictating solutions, the leader serves as a facilitator, encouraging individuals to identify and leverage their unique strengths to address challenges collaboratively. This was a challenge that my co-founders, Derrick Washington and Leslie Credle, and I had to face and overcome when building the No Longer 3/5th Coalition, as discussed in earlier examples.

One powerful example is the late Congressman John Lewis. John Lewis exemplified a coaching culture by empowering others to realize their potential and take action. Throughout the civil rights movement, he didn't simply lead. He mentored, listened, and created spaces where people from diverse racial, social, and economic backgrounds could unite around a shared purpose. He encouraged individuals to step into leadership roles, make decisions, and take risks in pursuit of justice, demonstrating that guidance and trust can unlock collective potential.

By fostering collaboration, amplifying voices, and nurturing resilience, Lewis built a movement that thrived on engagement and shared ownership rather than hierarchy. His work reflects the essence of a coaching mindset: creating an environment where people feel valued, supported, and capable of achieving more together than they could alone.

Finding My First Coach in the Unlikeliest Place

When we think about coaching, many of us imagine boardrooms, sports fields, or college campuses, places where mentors and leaders thrive. For me, my first real positive coach wasn't found in an office or on a college campus; it was in a prison cellblock. His name was Mac Hudson, and for those of you who have seen my TEDx talk (From Kingpin to Community Leader), you know this story well. Born in the streets of Roxbury, Boston, Mac once embraced that street lifestyle that ultimately landed him in prison in the early 1990s. Yet, while in prison, he ultimately overcame the very negative forces that once held me in bondage and dedicated his life to changing the lives of others.

Mac was the first person to show me what a coaching culture could look like, even in one of the most unforgiving environments imaginable. He wasn't a professional coach or a motivational speaker with accolades to his name. He was simply a man who saw potential in me when I couldn't see it in myself.

Long before I ever stood on stages or shared rooms with business, philanthropy, and coaching giants like Lee Pelton, Eric "ET" Thomas, Jeremy Anderson, Inky Johnson, Tony Robbins, Andrew Litchfield, Les Brown, and many others, I found myself at a fork in the road with this thing we call life, not knowing which way to go. In that prison cell, I was lost, drowning in my own thoughts, trapped by a mindset that had embraced criminality, not because I wanted to but because it felt like survival, a way of life I couldn't escape. Mac saw past that. He didn't just lecture me; he coached me.

He started by helping me understand my role as a Black man in America, a crucial step in rewiring a mindset shaped by years of trauma and limited perspectives. Mac gave me the tools to explore the historical journey of my people, from our roots in ancient Africa to our experiences in America. Setting me on a path of self-discovery. In other words, self-knowledge became the cornerstone of his approach.

I vividly remember one conversation when Mac looked me square in the eye and said:

"You have a gift that I've not seen many with, David. Trust me, I've met a lot of people in my time. You have this extraordinary ability, not only to bring people together but to inspire them to follow your lead. Imagine if you used that God-given gift to uplift communities and people, you'd be just as unstoppable in those areas as you have been in every other part of your life. Right now, you're using your gifts for the wrong things."

Those words stayed with me. Over time, they cut through the noise of my self-doubt and ignited something within me, a spark of worth and possibility I had never felt before.

That is what great coaches do. They see a version of you that you cannot yet see, and they refuse to stop speaking to that version of you.

Mac's coaching was relentless. He embodied what I call "Relentless Outreach": meeting a person exactly where they are and consistently showing up. No matter how many times I slipped, he was always there, patient and unwavering, coaching me with love and understanding, demonstrating that transformation is a long game.

Through countless, often uncomfortable yet transformational conversations, Mac challenged me to question my choices, to think critically about the impact of my actions, and to envision a future where I was more than my past mistakes. His unwavering belief in me laid the foundation for my shift from a survival mindset to one of purpose. It was his guidance that planted the seeds of integrity, accountability, and a passion for building up others and our communities, values I live by to this day.

What's powerful about a coaching culture is that it transcends environments. Whether you're in a corporate office, a nonprofit, a community center, or, as I was, a prison, coaching has the power to change lives. Mac equipped me with the tools to reject the life I once knew and to embrace one focused on transformation and positive leadership.

After thirty-two years behind bars, Mac is now home, doing exceptional community work in Boston as the founder of the nonprofit "AccessMa" and serving as the community liaison/paralegal for the Racial Equity in Corrections initiative for Prison Legal Services (PLS), working to change laws and policies that affect incarcerated individuals.

In the end, Mac Hudson wasn't just a coach; he was the embodiment of hope and resilience, not only for me, but for countless others, proving that even in the darkest places, a spark of guidance can illuminate the path to a brighter future.

Empowering Ownership, Inspiring Growth

At Motivational Dreamers, our strength lies not in my singular vision but in the heart and soul of our small, but incredibly powerful team. I've always believed that true leadership isn't about having all the answers; it's about creating an environment where every team member feels empowered to lead, grow, and share their unique gifts. This is the essence of our coaching culture.

What sets us apart is the way each member of our team takes ownership, as if Motivational Dreamers were their own brainchild. They don't just follow instructions; they contribute, challenge, and refine ideas continuously. Their commitment is so profound that I can confidently step back and trust that the day-to-day operations will run smoothly, freeing me to pursue new ventures and dedicate time to my main passion, youth empowerment work.

This coaching culture isn't just about meetings or structured sessions; it's a way of life here. It nurtures loyalty, inspires creativity, and builds resilience even when the road gets rocky. Every conversation, every piece of feedback, and every shared insight reinforces our collective strength. Our success is a testament to the power of coaching: by uplifting each other, we create a legacy of continuous growth and excellence.

At Motivational Dreamers, my team doesn't just run a company; we build a community, and, in doing so, we allow ourselves and me the freedom to dream bigger, knowing that our foundation is built on trust, empowerment, and shared purpose.

This is what a coaching culture looks like in real time. I do not just give orders; I ask questions, give feedback, and make space for my team to step up as leaders themselves.

Conclusion: The Ripple Effect of a Coaching Culture

In closing, a coaching culture is more than just a leadership approach; it is a powerful and transformative way of being. It's an intentional commitment that not only shapes organizations but also nurtures individuals, builds resilient relationships, fosters accountability, and unlocks hidden potential. In this chapter, we explored the core tenets of coaching: active listening, empathy, feedback, and empowerment. These tenets form the bedrock of a thriving, high-performing environment.

A true coaching culture is not simply a strategy to improve productivity or engagement; it is a framework for deep, lasting transformation across any context, whether in the streets, prison, corporate, or the nonprofit sector. The examples from my own life, from Mac Hudson's relentless outreach to the way Motivational Dreamers operates, serve as a testament to the real-world power of coaching. When you invest in people, listen to them, and challenge them to reach beyond their limitations, you create an ecosystem where all individuals can flourish, both personally and professionally.

By adopting these principles, leaders can cultivate an ecosystem where trust flourishes, innovation thrives, and organizations achieve sustainable success. However, the most profound impact occurs at the human level: individuals are not seen as just employees or team members; they are esteemed as human beings capable of greatness. A coaching culture meets people where they are, nurtures their growth, and encourages them to break through their internal barriers. The personal growth of others, shared moments of collaboration, and collective accountability are the true indicators of success in any endeavor.

This isn't just a blueprint for professional success; it's a legacy of leadership that touches lives, heals divides, and creates spaces for people to step into the fullness of their potential. When you build a coaching culture, you don't just empower individuals; you create movements that stretch beyond the boundaries of organizations and ripple across communities, industries, and society at large.

The call to action is clear: whether you're leading a small team or a global enterprise, look within yourself. Are you creating a culture based on trust, empathy, and growth? Are you choosing to respond to uncertainty with understanding and empowerment? When you lead with a coaching mindset, you equip those around you to succeed not just today but for generations to come. That is the legacy of true leadership, and when you answer the call, nothing is impossible.

Actionable Steps to Implement a Coaching Culture

1. **Educate Leaders and Teams:** Begin by training leaders in the principles of coaching, including active listening, asking powerful questions, providing constructive feedback, and fostering accountability. This isn't a one-time workshop; it's an ongoing commitment to learning. Offer certifications, role-playing sessions, and scenario-based training where leaders practice coaching conversations in real situations.

   Example: During a team project review, a leader might ask, *"What challenges did you encounter, and how did you overcome them?"* rather than immediately giving solutions. This approach encourages reflection, problem-solving, and ownership.

2. **Model Coaching Behavior:** Leaders must walk the talk. Demonstrate empathy, patience, and a growth-oriented mindset consistently.

   Example: If an employee misses a deadline, instead of focusing solely on the mistake, a coaching-oriented leader might say, "*Let's explore what challenges caused this and how we can prevent it next time.*" Modeling coaching behaviors signals that mistakes are learning opportunities and reinforces the value of development over perfection.

3. **Create Feedback Mechanisms:** A coaching culture thrives on open, honest communication. Establish multiple channels for feedback, from regular one-on-one check-ins to anonymous surveys and peer-to-peer feedback loops.

   Example: Weekly team huddles can include a segment where each member shares one area where they'd like coaching or support. Making feedback routine normalizes growth discussions and reduces fear of judgment.

4. **Integrate Coaching into Daily Practices:** Embed coaching into everyday interactions: performance reviews, team meetings, or casual check-ins. Leaders can set aside time in weekly meetings for "*growth moments*" where team members reflect on recent successes, challenges, and lessons learned.

   Example: In a nonprofit setting, after completing a community project, the leader could ask, "*What part of this project pushed you to grow, and how can we replicate that experience for others?*" Small, consistent coaching moments build a culture where development is part of the workflow, not an isolated event.

5. **Recognize and Reward Growth:** Acknowledgment reinforces coaching principles. Publicly celebrate milestones, learning breakthroughs, and examples of employees helping each other grow.

   Example: Tangible recognition could be a feature in a company newsletter highlighting a team member's growth, or internal awards like *"Coaching Champion of the Month."* This shows that the organization values not just results but how people develop and support one another along the way.

6. **Measure and Iterate:** Coaching culture isn't static; it evolves. Track the effectiveness of initiatives through surveys, engagement scores, retention metrics, or documented coaching interactions.

   Example: After implementing peer coaching, measure whether collaboration, team performance, or problem-solving metrics improve over the next six months. Use this data to refine approaches, celebrate progress, and address gaps. Iteration ensures the culture is actively nurtured and not assumed.

7. **Foster Peer Coaching:** Empower team members to coach one another, creating shared accountability and mutual growth. Pair employees for peer mentorship programs or establish small coaching pods where members rotate between roles of coach and learner.

Example: A junior staffer might coach a peer on time management while learning leadership techniques from another team member. Peer coaching strengthens relationships, reinforces learning, and multiplies the impact of leadership development across the organization.

Leadership Reflection

1. Do people around you feel developed, trusted, and empowered through your leadership, or simply managed and directed? What behaviors reveal the difference?

2. Reflect on a recent situation where you solved a problem for someone rather than helping them grow through it. How might a coaching mindset have changed the outcome?

List up to two ways you can help develop leadership in others.

1.

2.

A mentor is someone who allows you to see the hope inside yourself.

—Oprah Winfrey

CHAPTER 9

ANCHORED IN WISDOM — UNLEASHING THE POWER OF MENTORSHIP

What Is Mentorship?

Mentorship is not a casual friendship or an equal exchange of ideas where both parties start from the same place. It is not a free-for-all where anyone with a bit of insight becomes an instant guru, nor is it a shallow networking connection built solely on exchanging business cards. Mentorship is also not a one-way lecture or a rigid, formulaic process where the mentor simply dumps knowledge onto the mentee without understanding their unique journey.

At its core, mentorship is the deliberate act of sharing hard-earned wisdom, insight, and understanding that the mentee has yet to acquire. It is a relationship where the mentor, drawing from a deep reservoir of experience, illuminates the path ahead, offering guidance, opening doors, and sparking clarity where there was once confusion. The mentor's role is to bridge the gap between where you are now and where you aspire to be, providing you with the knowledge, strategies, and perspectives that only years of real-world experience can offer.

While both mentor and mentee can grow and benefit from the exchange, the relationship is fundamentally grounded in the mentor's responsibility to elevate the mentee. It's about transferring insights that transform obstacles into opportunities and challenges into stepping stones toward success. In this dynamic, the mentor is the seasoned guide, and the mentee is the eager learner, ready to absorb and apply these lessons to forge their own path toward leadership and achievements.

Why Mentorship?

Mentorship is the secret ingredient that accelerates your growth and transforms potential into reality. When you actively seek out a mentor, you're not just adding another contact to your network; you're inviting the seasoned wisdom of someone who has walked the path before you, someone who can illuminate the pitfalls and highlight the shortcuts along your journey.

The Benefits of Mentorship:

- **Accelerated Learning:** A mentor provides insights and perspectives that textbooks and theory simply can't offer. They share lessons honed by experience, mistakes made, battles fought, and victories won that help you avoid common pitfalls and fast-track your progress.
- **Enhanced Decision-Making:** With a mentor's guidance, you gain access to a well of practical advice and proven

strategies, allowing you to make more informed decisions. This helps you navigate complex situations with clarity and confidence.

- **Increased Accountability:** A mentor keeps you grounded and focused. They challenge you to set ambitious goals, hold you accountable to your commitments, and push you to step outside your comfort zone.
- **Expanded Networks:** Mentors often introduce you to key players in your industry, opening doors to opportunities that would otherwise remain out of reach. Their endorsement can provide the credibility needed to take your ideas to the next level.
- **Personal and Professional Growth:** Beyond business acumen, mentorship nurtures your emotional intelligence and leadership qualities. It instills resilience, fosters self-awareness, and cultivates the values of empathy and integrity, which are essential for lasting success.

The Consequences of Not Seeking Mentorship:

- **Stunted Growth:** Without the guidance of someone who has already navigated the challenging terrain of leadership, you may find yourself repeatedly reinventing the wheel, facing obstacles that could have been anticipated and managed more effectively.
- **Missed Opportunities:** A lack of mentorship can leave you isolated from valuable networks and insights. Opportunities to learn from those who have succeeded before you may vanish, causing you to miss out on connections that could catalyze your career.

- **Repeated Mistakes:** Without a mentor to provide perspective, the chance to learn from someone else's failures diminishes. This means that you may end up making the same mistakes, which can delay your progress and lead to unnecessary setbacks.
- **Limited Perspective:** The absence of mentorship can result in a narrow view of your industry or potential. A mentor challenges you to see beyond your current scope, encouraging innovative thinking and broadening your understanding of what's possible.
- **Increased Vulnerability:** Navigating the complexities of leadership without a mentor leaves you more exposed to errors and missteps that could otherwise be mitigated by seasoned advice.

In essence, mentorship isn't just an optional extra; it's a vital investment in your future. It transforms your journey from one of solitary struggle to a collaborative pursuit of excellence, empowering you to reach heights that might otherwise remain out of reach. It is the difference between wandering and being guided, between guessing and growing with intention. Embrace mentorship and unlock the door to wisdom, opportunity, and true leadership success.

Illuminating the Path: How Visionary Mentors Forge Leaders

In the fast-paced world of business, even visionaries like Mark Zuckerberg and Bill Gates recognize that no great leader achieves success alone. Take Mark Zuckerberg, for example. Though his journey with Facebook was marked by groundbreaking innovation, he openly acknowledged the inspiration he drew from Steve Jobs, a leader who redefined product design, intuition, and bold vision.

Jobs' approach to thinking differently not only ignited Zuckerberg's passion for innovation but also guided him as he navigated the challenges of scaling a global enterprise. Even without a formal mentorship arrangement, Jobs' influence underscored a simple truth: mentorship isn't solely about step-by-step guidance; it's about absorbing the mindset of a trailblazer and applying it in your own unique way.

My job is not to be easy on people. My job is to take these great people we have and push them and make them even better.

—Steve Jobs

Similarly, Bill Gates has often spoken about the profound impact of his relationship with Warren Buffett. Beyond sharing business insights, Buffett's mentorship helped Gates hone his strategic thinking and deepen his commitment to philanthropy. Gates learned that success isn't just measured in financial terms, but in the legacy of positive change you create for the world. Through Buffett's seasoned perspective, Gates was encouraged to look beyond immediate gains and embrace a broader vision, one that merges business acumen with social responsibility.

These examples illuminate a critical lesson: mentors are the catalysts who turn potential into performance. They provide you with a roadmap forged through their own trials and triumphs, allowing you to avoid pitfalls and seize opportunities that you might never see on your own. Whether through direct advice or the subtle yet powerful influence of a role model, mentorship enriches your leadership journey by teaching you how to innovate, persevere, and, ultimately, pay it forward.

If leaders at that level still lean on mentors, what makes any of us think we should try to navigate life and leadership alone?

When the Universe Speaks: Mentors Who Shaped My Destiny

Every step I took, whether on the tough streets of Bedford-Stuyvesant, in the disciplined corridors of Moriah Boot Camp, or within the transformative walls of prison, was guided by mentors uniquely suited to that moment in my life. In the streets, Rakim stepped in with a style that defied the norm, offering wisdom and guidance that went far beyond the harsh lessons of our environment. His mentorship wasn't about intimidation; it was about uplifting me and showing me a different way to lead, one built on respect and genuine care.

Later, at Moriah Boot Camp, military leaders drilled into me the value of discipline and accountability, often reminding us that excellence was nonnegotiable. I recall after one morning run, lungs burning, when a sergeant quietly walked alongside me and said, "The only person standing in your way is the one you see in the mirror." That standard of excellence became the bedrock of my leadership philosophy. Then, in prison, when hope was scarce and walls seemed to close in, Mac Hudson emerged as my first true coach. Through patient guidance and challenging conversations, he reshaped my thinking, igniting an awakening through self-knowledge and purpose I had never thought possible. Every lesson, every conversation, and every push to go further than I thought I could made me understand the real power of mentorship, not just in theory, but through lived experience.

I couldn't see it then, but each chapter of my life was perfectly orchestrated to send me the mentors I needed to prepare me for my higher calling: to inspire generations of leaders in classrooms, conference rooms, and beyond. As I stepped into the legitimate business world, the mentors of my past had served their purpose. They paved the way for the next level, a stage where the universe would send new mentors to guide me through uncharted territory: the business world.

Guided by Greatness: The Mentors Who Shaped My Journey

As I emerged from the lessons of the streets, prison, Moriah Boot Camp, and my experiences attending academic institutions, I stepped into the dynamic world of business. The wisdom I had accumulated became the bedrock of my journey as a founder, CEO, and community leader. Every real-life lesson about resilience, strategy, and leadership planted seeds that would later flourish into invaluable insights.

These early experiences were further refined through formal education and, more importantly, by the influence of extraordinary mentors. Icons like Dr. Eric "ET" Thomas and Jeremy Anderson, who ignited my passion for public speaking and consulting, have propelled my company to new heights. Tony Robbins, one of the greatest of all time, transformed my approach to business by personally teaching me how to discern and harness the underlying patterns that drive success through his business mastery methodology.

Yet, the journey didn't end there. I've always believed that even the most seasoned leaders need a coach in all areas of life. Andrew Litchfield of Penny Investments has guided me in confidently navigating complex property deals, while Ed Bastian's philosophies have reshaped my decision-making and leadership style. Countless others, including the luminaries mentioned above, enriched my life with wisdom that continuously challenges me to grow, adapt, and lead with purpose.

Mentors help you hone essential skill sets, and I've been blessed to share rooms and stages with some of the best. I would be remiss if I didn't give them their flowers; their influence has shaped not just the way I conduct business but the way I approach life. From these experiences, I developed a leadership philosophy that values trust, credibility, and ethical conduct above all else, including my mantra, "No man left behind," which means you take care of your people.

I remember when my speaking engagements and consulting were confined to top universities, youth organizations, summits, and the nonprofit space. I was doing well in those circles, but then a monumental opportunity arrived: a chance to speak at a Fortune 500 conference. The offer was huge, but so was my doubt. I questioned whether I was truly qualified to address a room full of elite leaders. Even someone as confident as I am can be gripped by uncertainty and insecurity.

I almost turned the opportunity down until I reached out to Jeremy Anderson, the Founder of the Next Level Speakers Academy. I jumped on a Zoom call with him, laying out my fears and hesitations. I'll never forget how intently he listened, and then, with calm conviction, he said:

"David, we're not turning down a wonderful opportunity like this. You are more than qualified; that's exactly why they chose you. But here's the thing: everyone can say you're qualified, but that means nothing if you don't believe it yourself.

This is your moment to level up, to bring a perspective to corporate America that's been missing. This is God's work, my brother. If you truly feel you have nothing to add, then don't do it, but we both know that's not the case. It's your time. You got this. Let's go."

That conversation marked a turning point, transforming my doubt into determination and courage. It pushed me into the corporate arena with renewed drive. I accepted the challenge, delivered a powerful presentation on "Leadership Responsibility" and nailed it, earning praise from top executives and opening doors I had only dreamed of. Since that defining moment, I have stepped onto some of the largest corporate stages. I have mentored executives, both professionally and personally, and built relationships in spaces a kid from the projects of Brooklyn could only imagine.

My journey has been anything but conventional, and I am profoundly grateful for every hardship and hard-won lesson that brought me to where I am today. The mentorship and guidance I received from these phenomenal leaders has left an indelible mark on my life. Their wisdom, combined with my lived experiences, continues to guide my work, shape my relationships, and fuel my commitment to leaving a lasting legacy of service, leadership, and meaningful impact.

I can say with all my heart that I am truly blessed and divinely favored, and much of that thanks goes to the mentors who believed in me when I doubted myself or couldn't yet see my purpose. Each of them not only honed my skills but also opened doors to opportunities I could have never imagined, allowing me to share stages and insights with some of the best in the industry. Their guidance is a constant reminder that leadership is a collective journey, one where the lessons of the past prepare us to inspire future generations. Today, I stand grateful and humbled, ready to pay it forward by empowering others to rise, lead, and succeed.

Conclusion: The Legacy Begins with You

The guidance of extraordinary mentors has illuminated every step of my journey. These mentors, whether they appeared in the form of a compassionate street leader, a disciplined military coach, or a visionary business strategist. They transformed my struggles into strength and my doubts into determination. Their wisdom has molded me into the leader I am today: a founder, CEO, and community leader, but above all, a man of faith who believes that true leadership is built not in isolation but in the collaborative dance of shared knowledge and unwavering support.

I stand before you, deeply grateful for every mentor who invested in my potential, who believed in me when I doubted myself, and who opened doors to opportunities I once thought were beyond my reach. Their lessons were not mere words; they were the catalysts that ignited a fire within me, a fire that propelled me to conquer challenges, to break through barriers, to find myself, and, ultimately, to inspire others along my path.

Now, I call upon you, dear reader, to embrace the transformative power of mentorship in your life. Seek those who have navigated the terrain before you, those who can share hard-earned wisdom that textbooks and theory cannot provide. Let their guidance help you overcome obstacles and seize opportunities with clarity and confidence. And when you have risen, when you have tasted the fruits of hard-won success, pay it forward. Become the mentor who lights the way for others, nurtures potential, and builds bridges in spaces once thought impenetrable. As Steven Spielberg wisely said, "The delicate balance of mentoring someone is not creating them in your own image but giving them the opportunity to create themselves."

This is your moment to step into a legacy of leadership, where every challenge becomes an opportunity to grow, and every mentor serves as a guiding light toward a future defined by purpose, resilience, and impact. Embrace mentorship not as a luxury but as a vital investment in your destiny. By doing so, you will not only transform your own journey but also empower an entire generation to rise, lead, and leave an indelible mark on the world.

The legacy of mentorship begins with you. Let's light the torch for tomorrow, today.

Actionable Steps for Securing the Right Mentor

1. **Reflect on Your Goals:** Begin by taking a deep look at your leadership journey and identifying areas where you need guidance.

   Example: Define your short- and long-term goals clearly. This self-reflection will help you understand what type of mentor can best support your growth. Knowing your strengths and weaknesses is the foundation for finding the right mentor.

2. **Identify Potential Mentors:** Research industry leaders, thought influencers, and professionals whose experiences align with your aspirations. I would suggest starting within your personal network, then working outward. Look for individuals whose values resonate with your own and who have demonstrated success in areas where you seek improvement.

   Example: Use professional networks, social media platforms, and industry events to compile a list of potential mentors. Their proven track record and alignment with your vision are key indicators that they can provide meaningful guidance.

3. **Initiate Thoughtful Outreach:** Reach out with a personalized message that highlights your goals and acknowledges their achievements. Be genuine in expressing why you believe their insights could be transformative for your journey. This first impression is crucial.

   Example: Demonstrate that you have done your research and explain how you envision their mentorship benefiting both of you. A respectful and well-articulated approach opens the door to a lasting mentorship relationship.

4. **Cultivate a Meaningful Relationship:** Once contact is established, commit to regular communication and actively seek feedback on your progress.

   Example: Ask insightful questions and share your challenges openly to create a dialogue that fosters growth. Show appreciation for their guidance by applying their advice and updating them on your achievements. This mutual engagement builds trust and transforms the mentorship into a dynamic, evolving partnership.

5. **Pay It Forward:** As you gain wisdom and experience, remember that mentorship is a two-way street. Share your insights and support others who are just starting their leadership journey. Embrace the idea that becoming a mentor is part of your growth process. By giving back, you not only honor your mentors but also contribute to a legacy of empowered leadership.

   Example: After gaining confidence and clarity through mentorship, a leader intentionally reaches back to support someone earlier in their journey. Instead of offering advice from a distance, they create consistent space for conversation, asking thoughtful questions, listening without judgment, and sharing lessons learned from real mistakes. Over time, that investment helps the next leader avoid common pitfalls, grow in confidence, and eventually do the same for someone else. This is how mentorship becomes legacy, not through titles but through continuity.

Leadership Reflection

1. Reflect on the mentors, coaches, or influential figures who have shaped your life and leadership. What lessons, conversations, or examples from them deeply impacted you most?

2. As you reflect on your own journey, who are you currently mentoring, inspiring, guiding, or encouraging? What kind of leadership legacy are you creating through your investment in others?

3. What is one leadership lesson you can pass on to someone else?

A legacy is etched not in a monument but in the lives we touch.

—David Baxter

CHAPTER 10

LEAD BEYOND YOURSELF — THE LAW OF LEGACY

By the time you arrive at mastery of your own leadership, the next question becomes unavoidable: What now? What is the purpose of the power, influence, and success you have fought so hard to achieve if it exists only for yourself? Leadership is not complete when it is inward-facing; it finds its highest calling when it lifts others.

For me, this lesson didn't arrive in a boardroom or in a polished seminar. It came in the everyday grind in Boston after my release from prison. Regular community and political events, networking and meeting new people, walking the streets, meeting youth where they were, and showing up consistently when no one else did. I remember countless afternoons sitting with young people who had no blueprint for success, helping them navigate the world they inherited, listening when no one else would, challenging them when they needed it most.

It was in these moments, the raw, unfiltered day-to-day work, that I realized leadership is less about titles or accolades and more about presence, guidance, and creating pathways where none exist.

Legacy in the Community

I didn't know it then, but those quiet afternoons with no cameras, no awards, and no guarantees were laying the foundation for everything that came after. These early moments shortly after my release paved the way for a greater impact. However, leadership beyond oneself is not about a single program or a single act. It is about a mindset, a commitment to use whatever success we attain to expand the horizons of others.

Whether it was working with state and city leaders to reform policies for formerly and currently incarcerated individuals, my work with the Partakers organization or Brandeis University to teach financial literacy and guide students back into higher education, or dedicating time to Roca, Inc., whom I still work with today, which disrupts violence and incarceration by working with the state's highest-risk youth. These experiences shaped my philosophy.

I learned that leadership is reciprocal: sometimes the young men and women I mentored held me accountable just as much as I held them accountable. It was in this work that the true meaning of legacy revealed itself: helping others rise, regardless of the resources or accolades available to me at the time.

Legacy in the Corporate and Nonprofit Sector

Legacy in business and nonprofit leadership is not defined by corner offices, board seats, or press releases. It is defined by the impact you leave on the people, teams, and systems you touch. Every decision, every hire, and every program you champion is an opportunity to extend your influence far beyond yourself. The true measure of leadership is not profit margins or annual reports; it is the growth, empowerment, and success of those you lead.

The leaders who leave a lasting legacy see beyond the immediate. They understand that mentoring a young manager today can shape the executives of tomorrow. They know that investing in culture through recognition, guidance, and accountability creates lasting impact that lasts long after they've moved on.. Legacy-oriented leaders do not hoard knowledge, opportunity, or influence. They distribute it with intention, building both the structures and the people who can carry the mission forward.

One live example of this principle in action is Marc Benioff, CEO of Salesforce, and his groundbreaking 1-1-1 model. This system is deceptively simple but profoundly transformative:

- **1% Equity:** Salesforce donates 1% of its company equity to charitable causes, allowing the company's growth to directly fuel social impact.
- **1% Product:** 1% of the company's products are donated to nonprofits and educational institutions, empowering organizations to operate more effectively without prohibitive costs.

- **1% Employee Time:** Employees dedicate 1% of their working hours to volunteerism, embedding a culture of giving into the company's DNA.

This is more than philanthropy; it's a structural commitment to legacy. Benioff didn't just write a check or host a gala; he created a system where success amplifies generosity, engages employees, and strengthens communities simultaneously. The ripple effects of this model endure far beyond any single project or year, proving that legacy is not a gesture; it is a framework. It's not an event; it is architecture. It is how you wire your success so that it automatically serves others.

In high-performing organizations, whether corporate or nonprofit, this same principle holds. Teams that feel supported, challenged, and valued produce better outcomes, innovate faster, and sustain progress through inevitable challenges. Nonprofits that prioritize developing their staff and empowering communities multiply their reach and strengthen systemic impact. Corporate leaders who lead beyond themselves build companies that endure, not just profit today but shape markets, culture, and industry standards for decades to come.

At its core, legacy in leadership is moral, strategic, and actionable. It is about designing your influence so that it does not end with your tenure. It is about creating pathways for others to thrive, making room for rising leaders, and ensuring the work you started continues to grow, scale, and evolve. When executed with intention, legacy becomes immortal, not in statues, awards, or recognition but in the lives, careers, and communities forever changed by your choices.

Other Giants Who Understand This Philosophy

This philosophy isn't just reflected in my own life; it's lived by leaders around the world who recognize this moral responsibility.

Melinda Gates has committed billions through the Gates Foundation, working to improve global healthcare, uplift women and girls, and expand access to education and opportunity worldwide. Her leadership is rooted in removing barriers, especially for those the system often leaves behind.

Warren Buffett has pledged to give away more than 99% of his wealth through initiatives that fight poverty, fund education, and support public health globally. But it's not just his generosity; it's his challenge to other billionaires to do the same that turns wealth into a vehicle for legacy.

LeBron James didn't just dominate the court; he built The I PROMISE School in Akron, Ohio, offering free tuition, meals, and wraparound support services to at-risk students and families. He understood that real influence isn't just stats; it's changing what a child believes is possible.

Jeremy and **Traci Anderson** are living proof that legacy is global. In Cape Town, South Africa, they provide full scholarships and partner with colleges to create educational opportunities for students who would otherwise be left behind. They're feeding entire communities, creating access, and changing lives one student, one family at a time.

However, the reality is that leadership and impact don't always require a massive platform.

Dashine Moore founded **Beat the Streets 413 Youth Inc.,** a basketball and mentorship program serving youth of all ages in Berkshire County, Massachusetts. Mr. Moore started Beat the Streets with little more than a basketball, a dream, and a heart for the youth. Today, it's expanding statewide.

Mac Hudson is the founder of **AccessMa**. With limited resources, he's created real impact in Boston's underserved communities through toy drives, back-to-school supply events, clothing drives, and neighborhood-wide giveaways.

Leadership is not measured by net worth; it's measured by action.

The Legacy Continues

A lot has changed since those early days walking Boston's streets and mentoring with no roadmap. Only faith, grit, and consistency.

When I first came home, my leadership didn't come with a title or a team. It looked like navigating Boston's streets, showing up in reentry programs, and teaching in classrooms. Mentoring youth and young adults. Building a name in Boston's political landscape, frontlining reforms. I had no nonprofit, no company, no powerful network at this time. Just a vision, some grit, and a belief that leadership meant showing up and lifting others.

Over time, that vision grew, and from those roots, it became something bigger than I could have ever imagined.

Today, my legacy-building work continues in new forms, but the philosophy remains unchanged. Education has always been at the core of my legacy. My mother dedicated her life to the education of others and herself, and instilled its importance in me.

Even now, I continue to pursue degrees and certifications. I am a nonstop, lifelong learner. Inspired by her example and in honor of her, I created the Janie Baxter Legacy Scholarship, which provides underserved young men and women with the opportunity to attend college, something I know can change the trajectory of their lives.

Motivational Dreamers has now expanded nationally. To give you a snapshot, here is what legacy in motion looked like in just one recent year. Our philanthropic arm, in 2024, hosted ten coat drives across seven cities in four states, five turkey drives in four cities across three states, and ten toy drives in six cities across four states. We contributed over $150,000 in charitable donations to nonprofits and awarded three full college scholarships and four partial scholarships to deserving students in the United States.

We have recently taken our philanthropic reach internationally to the shores of South Africa, and we are excited about the work being done there. Each initiative reflects the same principle: lifting others, creating opportunity, and leaving a tangible impact. We've already surpassed our 2024 stats in 2025, and it is my hope to double our 2025 stats to even more in 2026.

Let's be clear: These are not just numbers; they are families warmed, tables filled, and futures funded.

I still make time to speak at colleges, K-12 schools, and organizations across the country. I pour into students, staff, and communities, providing workshops, mentorship, and inspiration. This is where the real work lives, breathing life into the younger generation who will carry your philosophies, your ideas, and your wisdom forward to the next generation. This is how a legacy extends beyond yourself.

This is what it looks like now.

But it started with presence. It started with purpose.

And it continues with legacy.

Closing Call

Every law in this book was never meant to stop with you. From honoring your word, to recognizing others, to coaching and mentoring, each one was preparing you for this: to live a life that outlives you.

So, ask yourself: When you have "made it," when the applause quiets and the room empties, what will remain? Accolades? Or the countless lives you've touched, the opportunities you've created, and the hope you've delivered? True leadership leaves a footprint bigger than yourself. True leadership ensures your rise is not solitary but a platform for others to ascend.

This is the law of legacy: lead beyond yourself, and let the impact you create echo long after you've left the room.

Last Actionable Step: Your Turn to Lead Beyond Yourself

You've learned the laws.

You've read the stories.

You've seen what it looks like to lead from the inside out.

Legacy doesn't start when you "arrive"; it starts with one choice to lift someone else as you climb. It starts when you stop asking, "What do I get?" and start asking, "Who gets better because of me?"

The uncommon leader doesn't just rise.

They bring others with them.

And now?

It's Your Turn to Lead Beyond Yourself!

Leadership Reflection

1. When your leadership journey is over, what do you hope your legacy will be?

People join because of the inspiring vision; people depart because of poor leadership.

—David Baxter

CONCLUSION

EMBRACING THE LEADER WITHIN

Journey of the Uncommon Leader

As we reflect on the ten laws of leadership, one truth becomes abundantly clear: leadership is not a destination; it's a lifelong journey of growth, learning, and transformation. Rarely is it linear. It's marked by setbacks, challenges, and unexpected detours. Yet on that same path, you encounter moments of profound realization, insights that shift everything. These experiences have shaped me, refined me, and guided me toward becoming the leader I am today. And through these shared lessons, I hope to inspire your own journey of becoming.

From the streets of Brooklyn to standing on some of the biggest stages across our nation and leading in conference rooms of all kinds, my path of leadership has been far from traditional. It's been filled with victories and failures, confidence and doubt. Yet through every phase, one truth remained constant: leadership is not about perfection; it's about resilience, adaptability, and the courage to grow from every experience.

These laws are more than abstract ideas; they are the foundation of a leadership style that transcends settings and industries. They equip you to connect with and inspire others, whether you're motivating a team, mentoring a student, leading in a boardroom, or leading your community.

The ten laws we've explored in this book:

- Leading with Purpose
- Mastering Communication
- Celebrating Success
- Honoring Commitments
- Maintaining Moral Courage
- Practicing Active Listening
- Embracing Failure
- Developing Others to Lead
- Anchoring in Wisdom
- Leading Beyond Yourself

Each chapter draws from lived experiences, showing how these laws play out in real time. From environments where survival depended on instinct to spaces where strategy and vision shaped outcomes, these laws became my compass. Their consistency and adaptability anchored me through uncertainty.

The Interconnected Nature of Leadership

Each of these laws stands on its own, yet they are deeply interconnected. You cannot lead with purpose without first mastering communication. You cannot truly celebrate success without honoring your commitments. Active listening reveals your team's needs and transforms failure into growth. At the core of it all lies mentorship.

Leadership is about balance, knowing when to challenge and when to support, when to step forward and when to step aside. It requires adapting to the moment while remaining grounded in your values.

Transformational Leadership

Communication isn't one-size-fits-all, and neither is leadership. What works for one person won't always work for another. It's your responsibility to know when to apply the right approach. That requires understanding your team as individuals but also as a collective. It takes time, but the payoff is worth it.

As we close this journey, I want to leave you with what I believe is the highest expression of leadership: ***Transformational Leadership.*** That's what these ten laws prepare you for, not just a title or position but a movement.

Transformational leadership isn't about simply sharing information or managing tasks. It's about igniting a spark that transforms the way people think, feel, and act. It creates a shared vision that rallies hearts and minds. It inspires innovation, cultivates loyalty, and builds a foundation of trust and purpose. At its core, it requires every element of the ten laws we've explored. Together, these principles prepare you to lead with conviction, clarity, and compassion.

This concept was first articulated by James MacGregor Burns in his groundbreaking work, *Leadership*, where he described transformational leadership as *"a process in which leaders and followers raise one another to higher levels of morality and motivation."* Unlike transactional leadership, which relies on simple exchanges of rewards and consequences, transformational leadership transcends.

It speaks to our shared humanity, appealing to higher values and a deeper sense of purpose. It moves people to look beyond themselves and align with something greater.

Transformational leaders inspire their teams not through power or authority but by example, by embodying integrity, vision, and unwavering belief in what is possible. They challenge the status quo and invite their teams to think critically, dream boldly, and create courageously.

Respect and care are not just outcomes; they are the lifeblood of the culture these leaders foster. And here's the truth: this isn't a gift some are born with. It's a skill anyone can develop through dedication, practice, and a commitment to growth.

The ten laws of leadership are your foundation for this transformation. They are your guide to becoming a leader who doesn't just manage but also inspires—a leader who doesn't just direct but uplifts. By embodying these principles, you will not only lead more effectively; you will also grow as a person.

You will become someone who others look to, not because they have to, but because they want to. As John Quincy Adams so beautifully put it, *If your actions inspire others to dream more, learn more, do more, and become more, you are a leader.*

As you finish this book, reflect on your own leadership journey. Where are you now? Where do you want to go? Who do you need to become in order to lead at the next level? Which of the ten laws spoke to you most? How will you apply them personally and professionally?

The road to great leadership isn't always easy. But it's worth it. When you lead with authenticity and courage, you don't just create change; you become the change.

Leadership isn't about where you come from; it's about where you're headed and who you uplift along the way. Take these laws with you. Live them. Build on them. Refine them. Make them your own.

As a leader, your job is not to be the hero of the story but to help others become heroes in their own story. This is also known as servant leadership. It is the ability to elevate yourself and those you lead to new heights of performance, collaboration, and purpose. It creates a ripple effect of positive change that spreads across individuals, teams, and communities.

While this kind of leadership is rewarding, make no mistake that it demands effort. It requires courage to embrace challenges, humility to learn from them, authenticity to connect deeply, and empathy to lead with heart.

Transformational leadership is not a destination but a lifelong journey; it is not a tool you wield but a craft you master, a way of leading that makes a profound and lasting difference. By living out the ten laws of leadership, you hold the power to shape not only your organization but also the world around you.

My own journey is proof: transformational leadership lifted me out of survival mode and into purpose, and now it's the framework I use to lift others.

This is your moment, step into it boldly. Lead with vision, communicate with purpose. Become the transformational leader you were always meant to be. The world is waiting for you.

This is the journey of the uncommon leader, and yours is just beginning.

ABOUT THE AUTHOR

David Baxter is a philanthropic entrepreneur, investor, and award-winning speaker dedicated to helping organizations and individuals achieve meaningful, measurable growth. As a philanthropist, he advances educational and community initiatives that expand opportunity and create pathways to long-term success for underserved communities around the world. As an entrepreneur and investor, he builds and supports ventures aligned with innovation, leadership, and impact.

He is the Founder and CEO of David Baxter & Associates, a national consulting and speaking firm, as well as Dreamers Media, a media and publishing company.

Born and raised in Brooklyn, New York, David now works nationally and internationally, delivering a message of leadership, accountability, and transformation to diverse audiences and institutions.

David has partnered with Fortune 100 companies, leading universities, nonprofits, and national conferences to equip leaders with practical strategies to navigate complexity, strengthen culture, and improve performance. His work focuses on building leadership capacity and driving results that extend beyond inspiration into execution.

As one of the most sought-after voices in leadership and organizational development, David has been featured on Boston 25 News, FOX, CityLine on Channel 5 Boston, and in multiple national publications, where he shares insights on leadership, culture, and organizational transformation. He is also a member of ForbesBLK, a global community of leaders advancing innovation, collaboration, and economic equity.

David's academic background includes studies at Emerson College, the University of Michigan, and the Massachusetts Institute of Technology (MIT). He is currently pursuing a Master of Science in Leadership and a doctorate in Education at Merrimack College; these experiences, combined with his professional practice, enable him to bridge theory with real-world execution across industries.

David's work is grounded in both personal experience and professional expertise, offering a perspective that connects leadership principles with actionable strategy. His message is clear: leadership is not defined by title, but by responsibility, consistency, and results.

For organizations seeking a speaker and consultant who delivers both vision and execution, David Baxter provides a proven approach to leadership and culture that drives lasting impact.

www.davidbaxterspeaks.com

www.davidbaxterbooks.com

BIBLIOGRAPHY

Gallup. "Why Trust in Leaders Is Faltering and How to Gain It Back." *Gallup Workplace Report*, April 17, 2023. https://www.gallup.com/workplace/473738/why-trust-leaders-faltering-gain-back.aspx.

Bonusly. "Employee Appreciation Survey: Statistics and Trends." *Bonusly*, 2023. https://bonusly.com/post/employee-appreciation-survey.

BIBLIOGRAPHY

www.ingramcontent.com/pod-product-compliance
Lightning Source LLC
LaVergne TN
LVHW010546160826
845677LV00013B/3020

* 9 7 9 8 9 9 5 7 7 0 3 0 5 *